Strike the Match
Light the Fire

Other Books by Kathleen S. Evenhouse

Less Than a Widow
Disable the Label
Discover Ruth

Praise for **Strike the Match, Light the Fire**

"What encourages me about this book, *Strike the Match, Light the Fire*, are the stories told within it. Why? The stories shared are true, for I know the story tellers and am mindful of the challenges they have faced as they sought to "strike the match" of faith through what is called "the chain reaction of praise." I was encouraged and strengthened as I reflected upon words thoughtfully written. I pray you will be too."
~ Kevin Korver, Senior Pastor, Third Church, Pella, IA

"If you don't want your spiritual life transformed, then put this book down and walk away! When Keith Korver first introduced our local gathering of Jesus followers to the simple spiritual blueprint that is now unpacked for everyone in *Strike the Match, Light the Fire*, I do not exaggerate in stating that it has been life-changing for both my wife and me. Every crisis, adversity, obstacle, failure, trial, and difficulty we have experienced since digesting the contents of this book has immediately become for us a "chain reaction of praise moment." For in each breaking point, we return to the simple, yet profound, principles contained in this book. Instead of getting mired in fear, worry, and anxiety, we immediately strike the match of praise and begin the active faith journey into the power of prayer, overcoming evil, and maturing toward the full realization of our true and eternal position in Christ."
~ Tom Vander Well, President & CEO at Intelligentics and prolific "Wayfarer" blogger and podcaster

"We live in a world that seems to be moving faster and faster with what seems like new twists and turns at every corner. Kathleen helps us to capture how we can navigate a challenging world through our faith in Jesus. I love how they take the reader through those stories of the past and show that they still apply today. When we stay full of faith, pray regularly, and praise the Father at every corner, things just don't seem as difficult. This book is a 'must read' for those of us who are trying to make sense out of this life while being obedient to what God has for us."
~ Jayson Henry, CEO at The Well, *Offering Help and Hope*

"Faith doesn't keep us out of trouble nor does it prevent bad things from happening, but it does help us get through them. But what do you do when your faith seems to drift away? In *Strike the Match, Light the Fire,* author Kathleen Evenhouse provides thoughtful ideas for getting through hard times and help make sense in a world gone crazy."

~ Dirk Wierenga, Author, Documentary Filmmaker, and Photographer

Strike the Match
Light the Fire

to step into a God-given chain reaction
and live what you believe

Kathleen S. Evenhouse

Strike the Match, Light the Fire
© 2021 by Kathleen S. Evenhouse
Published by Writing With Vision, Pella, IA

ISBN 978-1-7375955-0-2

All rights reserved. No portions of this publication may be reproduced, stored in a retrieval system, or transmitted in any form or by any means—electronic, mechanical, photocopy, recording, or any other—except for brief quotations in printed reviews without the prior permission of the publisher.

Scripture refernces are taken from the following resources: New Living Translation, marked (NLT), copyright ©1996, 2004, 2015 by Tyndale House Foundation. Used by permission of Tyndale House Publishers, Carol Stream, Illinois 60188. All rights reserved. THE MESSAGE, marked (MSG) copyright © 1993, 2002, 2018 by Eugene H. Peterson. Used by permission of NavPress, represented by Tyndale House Publishers. All rights reserved. New International Version®, marked (NIV)®. Copyright © 1973, 1978, 1984, 2011 by Biblica, Inc.™ Used by permission of Zondervan. All rights reserved worldwide. www.zondervan.comThe "NIV" and "New International Version" are trademarks registered in the United States Patent and Trademark Office by Biblica, Inc.™ The Passion Translation®, marked (TPT). Copyright © 2017, 2018 by Passion & Fire Ministries, Inc. Used by permission. All rights reserved. The Holy Bible, English Standard Version®, marked (ESV), copyright © 2001 by Crossway, a publishing ministry of Good News Publishers. Used by permission. All rights reserved."

Printed in the United States of America
Cover Design: Kathleen S. Evenhouse
  with background photo by Wes Hicks on Unsplash
Interior Design: Kathleen S. Evenhouse
Photos by Scott Platt

www.kathleensevenhouse.com
email author at KSEvenhouseWWV@gmail.com

Praise God from whom all blessings flow!

With thanks to
our spouses for their support
and to our test class participants
for their input.

Contents

Preface by Keith Korver	XI
• Chapter 1: Strike the Match; Light the Fire •	15
• PART 1: PRAISE •	23
Chapter 2: Story Time, Past and Present	25
Chapter 3: What Are You Wearing?	37
Chapter 4: Let the Praises Begin	49
• PART 2: FAITH •	61
Chapter 5: Story Time, Past and Present	63
Chapter 6: God's Gift of Faith	71
Chapter 7: Aim It! Flame It!	81
• PART 3: PRAY POWERFUL PRAYERS •	95
Chapter 8: Story Time, Past and Present	97
Chapter 9: What Is Prayer?	109
Chapter 10: Power Through Prayer	125
• PART 4: OVERCOME EVIL •	145
Chapter 11 Story Time, Past and Present	147
Chapter 12: At War with Evil	157
Chapter 13: Onward, Christian Soldiers	171
• PART 5: REIGN & RULE WITH CHRIST •	185
Chapter 14: Story Time, Past and Present	187
Chapter 15: You Just Thank the Lord	201
Chapter 16: Bearing Fruit in the Kingdom of God	213

• Chapter 17: God's Provision: A Chain Reaction •	229
• **APPENDICES** •	237
A: The Circle of Love	239
B: Leader Guide	243
C: The Order of Salvation	249
D: The Will of God	253
• **INDEX OF SCRIPTURE TEXTS** •	255

Preface

BY KEITH KORVER

Strange and unusual things often happen in our lives that put us in places and positions we neither dreamt of nor even wished for. So, here I am, a non-writer attempting to write something worth reading, (Praise the Lord I have a very capable co-author.) As the inspired prophet communicated the word of the Lord in Isaiah 55, he conveyed God's perspective: His ways and thoughts are so much higher than ours, and He lifts us up from the minutiae of our small perceptions and perspectives of reality into the greater realm of life in the Spirit (John 14:23-26). It is in that spirit that we attempt to share what the Lord has put on our hearts.

In Ecclesiastes, King Solomon shares a truth that *"What has been will be again, what has been done will be done again; there is nothing new under the sun....and of the making of many books there is no end, and much study wearies the body. Now all has been heard; here is the conclusion of the matter: Fear God and keep his commandments, for this is the whole duty of man. For God will bring every deed into judgment, including every hidden thing, whether it is good or evil"* (Ecclesiastes 1:9, 12:11-14).

What follows is simply a retelling of a spiritual warfare discipline as old as the early church fathers and mothers in the Christian faith.

A number of years ago, a friend of mine gave me his deceased mother's library of Christian books. This kind of thing has happened in my past twice before, so I resigned myself to disposing of books that someone else could not bring themselves to do. To be fair, my friend and the wishes of his mother were that a pastor would receive her library. I laid all the books out on several tables, and I asked the Holy Spirit which of them he wanted me to keep and digest. Here is where an unusual thing occurred. As I read the titles and descriptions, two of the books seemed to pop, reverberating and lifting in an unusual way to my eyes. Immediately, Hebrews 4:12 came to mind:

> *The word of God is living and active. Sharper than any double-edged sword, it penetrates even to dividing soul and spirit, joints and marrow; it judges the thoughts and intentions of the heart. Nothing in all creation is hidden from God's sight. Everything is uncovered and laid bare before the eyes of him to whom we must give account.* (Hebrews 4:12, NIV)

It was a "visual" *rhema* (God-spoken) moment where I believe the Lord communicated to me that he wanted me to read two specific books out of the lot. So that is what I did.

One of these designated books was written by Dr. Paul Billheimer, *Destined for the Throne: How Spiritual Warfare Prepares the Bride of Christ for Her Eternal Destiny* (Bethany House Publishers Minneapolis, MN 1975/revised 1996). In his work, Dr. Billheimer relied heavily on the Apostle Paul's New Testament letters to the Ephesian and Roman churches which urges spiritual preparation for eternity.

As I read, a pattern lifted to the surface: an actual and explicit chronological ordering of how the Holy Spirit leads us when we put a "chain reaction of praise" into practice. It became clear to me that practicing this God-given sequence will bring us to greater spiritual authority in our lives now.

I want to acknowledge another author who was very formative in this spiritual journey. In his seminal work, *Four Keys to Hearing God's Voice* (Destiny Image Publishers, Shippensburg, PA 2010), Dr. Mark Virkler emphatically teaches that spiritual disciplines must be developed in a believer's life. Why? So that we can receive and grow in an actual transformational relationship with the living Triune God who is always communicating with us. We can transform our ways of thinking, hearing, and operating "in the Holy Spirit" through the renewing of our minds (Romans 12:2). He always reminds his students that the Bible is meant to be actually lived out, by faith, in our daily experience of life.

Noted author Derek Prince said, "The Bible is a book of examples, not of exceptions as we often treat it." Go back to your Bible, and you will find that it is full of examples of people whose *faith and actions worked together, whose actions made their faith complete in their everyday lives* (James 2:22).

"Live your faith" is the theme of this book. It encourages us to "do the Bible" in our everyday lives, to understand in hope that we can be victorious overcomers in our lives now through a chain reaction that begins with praise. Join us, and we'll keep learning together.

This chain reaction of praise is another spiritual weapon that God has provided to add to the spiritual armor inventory He gave us in Ephesians 6: 10-19. I pray that you are inspired to participate in the flowing sequence explained in this book and keep the goal in mind!

> When we PRAISE the Lord God,
>
> Our FAITH IS ACTIVATED,
>
> To PRAY to release God's power and authority,
>
> So that we can OVERCOME EVIL,
>
> And RULE AND REIGN with Jesus Christ in victory now and forever.

CHAPTER 1

Strike the Match Light the Fire

Praise starts a chain reaction in which God supplies all we need as we walk in obedience and relationship with Him.

Have you ever reached a point where you couldn't grab hold of your faith?

- Your teenager left home.
- You lost your job and can't pay your bills.
- Your marriage is falling apart, and you wonder where the love went.
- You are suffering with chronic health issues.
- Your children wandered from the faith and are raising your grandchildren without God.
- Your fiancé had a change of mind a week before the wedding.
- You've been trying for years, without success, to have a child.
- You did something you can't forgive yourself for.
- Life is overwhelming, and depression takes a firm grip on you.
- You are waiting—still waiting—for God's blessings to pour out and the hard stuff to end.
- Why did your loved one have to die?

The Bible gives us examples of others who—like us—felt desperately alone and in pain.

- Job lost everything, was covered with painful boils, and sat in an ash heap (Book of Job).

- Ruth, childless and widowed, was an outcast immigrant in her new country (Ruth 1-4).
- David, who was hiding for his life, sunk into deep depression (Psalm 32:1-4).
- A woman had chronic bleeding, and the best physicians could not help her (Luke 8:43-48).
- Mary and Martha pleaded for Jesus to save their brother Lazarus, but he died (John 11).
- Judas Iscariot betrayed his rabbi Jesus for 30 pieces of silver (Matthew 26-27).
- Mary Magdalene was broken with anguish when her rabbi was crucified and buried. Then she discovered that his body was not in the tomb (Mark 16).

Does any of this sound familiar? If so, please keep reading—this study is for you. God not only knows you, your situation, and your feelings, He has provided a pathway to faith and peace for each of us. It's not a formula for which you have to find the strength to enact each step on your own. Instead, it is a chain reaction that you choose to initiate, and God flows it from there. He has already made provision for your faith, His power and authority, and His peace to flow through you all day, every day.

We live in a broken world powerfully influenced by Satan. Life can be very hard, indeed, but it is never hopeless.

> *For this is how God loved the world: He gave his one and only Son, so that everyone who believes in him will not perish but have eternal life. God sent his Son into the world not to judge the world, but to save the world through him.* (John 3:16-17, NLT)

Jesus defeated sin and death, rose from the grave, and sits at the right hand of the Father in heaven (Acts 2:33). Our sins died with Him, and we rise with Him in victory. We are no longer slaves to sin, but are heirs of God, part of His family, and invited into close relationship with Him (Romans 1:15-21). Not only that, the

Counselor—the Holy Spirit—now lives on earth in the hearts of all those who believe (John 14:26).

Even so, sometimes we may feel separated from God, attacked, in pain, broken, or afraid. Our sin builds roadblocks in our relationship with God, and we miss our way, get lost, and can't find our way back. The great news is: God is always there and desires us to be with him (James 4:8).

God provides all the tools, protection, and help that we need to live in His Kingdom on earth. We just need to strike a match against earth's rough surface by praising God every day in every circumstance. He already has the fire of faith laid and waiting for one tiny spark to burst into flames. It begins a chain reaction to enable us to access that which God has already set in place in each of us.

WHAT IS A CHAIN REACTION?

A chain reaction is scientific term for a series of events so closely related that each action brings about the next one. Let's restate this important concept: In a chain reaction, each step causes the next step, which causes the next step and the next, until there is one long chain of events.

Fire is a good example of a chain reaction. An initial spark begins the chain reaction, as in striking a match and holding its flame to kindling. However, three things are needed for a fire to burn: fuel, air (oxygen), and heat (which continues the process). Once burning, a fire's uninhibited chain reaction provides gases (produced by heat) that add fuel to maintain the fire.

How do you stop a fire? Weaken any one of the three necessary items, and the fire will weaken. Strengthen any one or more of the elements, and the fire will increase in intensity. Remove any one of the three, and the fire will cease to burn. You can be sure the devil knows the details about how this spiritual chain reaction operates and uses this knowledge in his attempts to deceive us and separate us from God.

The Holy Spirit appeared on earth as a tongue of fire above the heads of the disciples in the upper room. The flame of the Spirit ignited a spiritual change in these Christ-followers, transforming their faith from quiet embers into a roaring fire, and they spread the gospel throughout the world.

We use the chain reaction of fire in this book to illustrate a spiritual renewal pattern that each of us can integrate into our daily lives. Modeled in the Bible, this chain reaction helps Christians grow beyond mere head knowledge to Godly action, which flows from a strong, on-going relationship with God (John 15:5).

> *What I'm getting at, friends, is that you should simply keep on doing what you've done from the beginning ... live in responsive obedience ... keep it up. Better yet, redouble your efforts. Be energetic in your life of salvation, reverent and sensitive before God. That energy is God's energy, an energy deep within you, God himself willing and working at what will give him the most pleasure.* (Philippians 2:12-13, MSG)

The verses above describe sanctification, the process of moving into holiness, of gaining the character of Jesus. It's a work of both God and man (Galatians 6:2-10).

How does this relationship with God work? God shows us a pattern, lays the groundwork, and marks the pathway to transformation and relationship. This connection began when we chose Jesus Christ as our Lord and Savior, and it continues as we make a daily choice to praise God. When we struggle, the Holy Spirit reminds, encourages, and overshadows us so that our circumstances turn from disaster to invitations from Him to step forward holding His hand. As we turn to look at God instead of our pain, He fills us and enables us to praise Him in spite of our weakness. And that praise starts the chain reaction in which God supplies all we need as we walk in obedience and relationship with Him.

STRIKE THE MATCH OF PRAISE

It only takes a spark to get a fire going, and praise is that spark. When we choose to look at God, even if our world may be falling apart around us, praise changes our focus from the problem to the Almighty. With this God-focus, our faith and hope are regenerated (Psalm 16:8-11), which causes the road blocks to faith such as guilt, fear, or pain to burn in the fire. God is always there for us, and praise ignites our faith in Him.

> *What a gift life is to those who stay the course! You've heard, of course, of Job's staying power, and you know how God brought it all together for him at the end. That's because God cares, cares right down to the last detail.* (James 5:11, MSG)

We strike the match of praise, and the kindling of our God-given faith bursts into flames. As the flames of Jesus' faith flare up in us, we can pray for God to release His power and authority to overcome evil in the authority of Jesus' name.

As a fire blazes, gases that are produced by heat provide a continual source of fuel. In this same way, we have the unending fire of the Holy Spirit burning in us, and we experience the faith of Jesus Christ (Colossians 3:4). Therefore, we have access to a continual flow of God's strength and power so that we can reign and rule in His Kingdom here on earth and in heaven for eternity.

Even if your fire is dying down and your cooling embers are buried deep, faith can be re-ignited with praise. And the chain reaction begins again.

> When we **praise** the Lord in all circumstances.
>
> Our **faith** bursts into flame and burns within us,
>
> So that we can **pray** to release God's power and authority
>
> To **overcome evil** in Jesus' name
>
> And **reign and rule with Christ** on earth and in heaven.

Explore and Exercise

1. Naomi and Elimelech were so affected by a lengthy famine in Bethlehem that they decided to move with their two young boys to Moab, where the rains were sufficient and food was available. Their plan was to stay only a few years among the idol-worshipping Moabites, just until the famine was over. However, their boys became men and Elimelech died, and the family was still in Moab. The sons married Moabite women and remained in the country that they viewed as home. When tragedy struck and her sons also died, Naomi could no longer hold onto her faith and traveled home to Bethlehem, hoping to die among her own people. As she arrived, everyone gathered around her and asked, "Could this be Naomi?"

   "Don't call me Naomi," she responded. "Instead, call me Mara, for the Almighty has made life very bitter for me. I went away full, but the Lord has brought me home empty. Why call me Naomi when the Lord has caused me to suffer and the Almighty has sent such tragedy upon me?" (Ruth 1:20-21, NLT)

   You can read the whole story in the Book of Ruth, just four chapters, in the Old Testament.

   a. As Naomi returned to Bethlehem, her mental and spiritual tank had hit rock bottom. Full of bitterness and pain, Naomi believed that God didn't care about her any more, and this separation from God left her without hope or a reason for living. If you recognize this emotion, if you have experienced doubt when in pain, if you have ever questioned whether or not God really loved you, briefly share your time in this dark place.

   b. Did you find your way back to faith? If so, what caused you to change course and return to this relationship with God?

2. Pretend you have a class of six-year-olds in front of you. Explain to them what a chain reaction is.

3. **Chain Reaction Challenge:** Followers of God know that transformation requires filling our minds with what is true, and honorable, and right, and pure, and lovely, and admirable (Philippians 4:8). We store things that we think are important in our memory, and those thoughts that we choose to fill our minds with are what shows up in our words and actions.

   The Chain Reaction of Praise is an important road map that shows us how to get to and maintain a close relationship with God. Memorize and review it often so that it stays in the front part of your brain for easy access when needed. Here are some suggestions to help you glue this process (also a tool and a weapon) in your minds and heart.

Chain Reaction of Praise

   a. Visualize striking a match and watch the fires flare up one by one as you go through the Chain Reaction of Praise. Each flame causes the next one to ignite until they are all alight and continue to burn.

> When we **praise** the Lord in all circumstances,
> (Revelation 4:11, Psalm 22:3, 8:2)
>
> Our **faith** is ignited and its fire burns in us,
> (Romans 12:3, James 5:16-17)
>
> So that we can **pray** for God to release His power and authority,
> (Psalm 37: 4-5, 1 John 5:14-15)
>
> To **overcome evil** in Jesus' name,
> (Luke 10:18-21, Philippians 2:12-13)
>
> And **reign and rule with Christ** on earth and in heaven.
> (Ephesians 1:13-14, 1:17-23, 2:6-7, 3:10-13)

b. Use your hand as a memorization tool, with thumb and fingers representing each of the five links in the chain.

c. Practice the "elevator speech" (based on the graphic on previous page) in preparation to bring your listener (in less than a minute) from no knowledge of this chain reaction to understanding the steps.

d. Those of you with engineering minds might want to place this chain reaction into a flow chart. Or if you have more of a creative bend; draw a picture that reveals what this chain reaction does in your life.

PART 1

PRAISE GOD

Praise is the shortest distance between you and God.

God will never leave us or forsake us (Deuteronomy 31:6), but there are times in this cold, cruel world that we experience blockades that oppose our close relationship with Him. These barriers might be fear, pain, guilt, circumstances, or worry. So many obstructions can dampen our faith fires, but God has given us a surefire chain reaction to reignite our faith and trust in Him.

Praise is the spark that ignites faith's flame and burns away the walls between us and God (Psalm 42:5).

We are not praising God FOR any of the broken situations which are part and parcel of living in a fallen world. Instead, we praise Him IN all circumstances, and this action strikes the match that begins a chain reaction. Paul wrote this from a Roman prison cell:

> *Be joyful always; pray continually; give thanks IN all circumstances for this is God's will for you in Christ Jesus.* (1 Thessalonians 5:16-18, NIV)

Praise sparks a chain reaction that fans the fires of faith, prayer, overcoming evil, and living in the Kingdom of God on earth as it is in heaven.

Praise God. This simple act can give you your heart's greatest desire—to know and to be known by your Creator! It opens your spiritual eyes and heart so that you can see Him for who He is. In turn, the Holy Spirit floods you with love so that you understand how precious you are to Him. As you delight in Him, you can feel Him delighting in you. He is brilliant!

~Vicki Koger, Praise and Prayer Warrior, March 2021

PART 1: CHAPTER 2

Story Time: Past and Present

Give thanks to the Lord; his faithful love endures forever! (2 Chronicles 20:21, NLT)

JEHOSHAPHAT

An Old Testament Story of a King Who Learned to Praise God

THE PREQUEL: HIS FAMILY'S CHECKERED PAST

Jeshoshaphat was the sixth king in David's family line, the family that God chose to eventually bring His Son into the world. You might think of these kings as outstanding heroes of faith, but they were still prone to sin like you and me. Still, God chose them to play a part in His Kingdom on earth.

If we had graphed the rhythms of their spiritual hearts during their lifetimes, we would have seen abnormal EKGs that warned of irregularities, impaired blood flow, disturbances, and damaging attacks. Here is a small sampling of the kings in David's family line: David was "a man after God's own heart," but even he exhibited spurts of impetuous, worldly behavior (1 Samuel 16:1 to 1 Kings 1).

- Solomon asked God for wisdom, but gradually shifted from dependence on God to relying on his own human wisdom (1 Kings 1-11).

- Rehoboam's actions divided God's people into two countries: ten tribes (Israel) named a new king and abandoned God, while the other two tribes (Judah) chose to follow God. As Judah's king, Rehoboam waffled between self-interest and faithful obedience. (2 Chronicles 10-12)

- Asa (Judah's king) walked with God, and God provided victory and peace for 35 years until Israel threatened their security (2 Chronicles 14:11). Asa then chose to rely on his own power and formed a human alliance using temple treasures as a bribe. When a prophet told him of God's displeasure, Asa severely punished the man and others. Later Asa later developed a serious illness, but sought only medical help rather than turning to God. He died bitter and angry. (1 Kings 15-16)

Do you see a pattern? When the kings stepped out of close fellowship with God, when they focused on worldly strength and self-importance instead, they and their countrymen had no help when disaster struck. EKGs of their spiritual hearts would have revealed ill health as they once again forgot God's truth.

WITHOUT FAITH, THE HEART FALTERS

2 Chronicles 20

Jeshoshaphat began his reign in faith: "He was deeply committed to the ways of the Lord." He sent Levites throughout Judah to teach the people about God, and God blessed Judah. The fear of the Lord fell on all the surrounding kingdoms so that none of them wanted to declare war on Jehoshaphat. Jeshoshaphat had fortresses and storage cities built throughout Judah and maintained a large, well-trained army.

However, with peace came complacency, and Jeshoshaphat strayed from his fellowship with God. He arranged the marriage of his son to wicked King Ahab's daughter, allying Judah with the Ba'al-worshipping kingdom of Israel. If he had taken a spiritual EKG, Jeshoshaphat would have been warned of an impending heart attack.

Ahab threw a huge all-you-can-eat barbecue in Samaria to celebrate the union. In the middle of the feasting and revelry, Ahab revealed his hidden agenda. "Dear friend Jeshoshaphat, won't you join me in a battle to regain territory for Israel?"

Jeshoshaphat promised, "You bet. I and my troops are with you all the way." He then remembered God and added, "But before we do anything, let's find out what the Lord says."

Ahab readily agreed, called for his 400 prophets, and asked their advice, "Should I attack Ramoth Gilead or hold back?" Naturally, these yes-men gave a convincing performance and promised an overwhelming victory.

The King of Judah still hesitated, "I think we need a second opinion. Isn't there a prophet of the Lord here?"

Ahab mentioned Micaiah, "Yes, but Micaiah never says anything good to me, only doom, doom, doom. I hate that guy!"

With a mild reproof for this un-kingly language, Jeshoshaphat insisted on calling on the prophet of God.

Micaiah first mocked the gang of prophets and told Ahab, "Go for it, King. You'll have an easy victory." So Ahab put on his own show and demanded that Micaiah speak only God's truth.

"I see Israel scattered over the hills as sheep without a shepherd. At God's command, his angels seduced you to desire this war, and he got all the prophets to lie to you promising victory," Micaiah prophesied. "See? God has pronounced your doom."

The 400 prophets jeered, and Ahab furiously ordered that Micaiah be imprisoned. As he was dragged away, the prophet voiced these parting words, "When you don't return from battle, everyone will see that God has spoken through me."

The kings prepared for war, but Micaiah's prophecy worried Ahab. He plotted to thwart God's plans for his doom, using Judah's king as a decoy. "Jeshoshaphat, old buddy, why don't you wear your kingly robes into battle. You'll look so fine and will inspire the men!" Ahab added slyly, "I think I'll go into battle in disguise so I can get up close and personal with my troops."

The Aramean charioteers had one order: "Kill Ahab!" Spotting kingly robes, they chased Jeshoshaphat until he convinced them he wasn't the King of Israel. But neither Ahab's disguise nor his armor could protect him from God. He was hit by a stray arrow and died by the end of the battle.

God's prophet Jehu confronted Jeshoshaphat on his return to Judah. "You have no business helping evil and loving those who hate the Lord! The wrath of God is on you, but He also recognizes the good in you, for you have committed yourself to seeking God and have led your people in cleansing the land."

Humbled, Jeshoshaphat repented and renewed his faith, leading the people of Judah in worshipping the God of their ancestors. He installed judges throughout the nation, charging them to: "Live in fear of the Lord—be most careful, for God hates dishonesty, partiality, and bribery. Be bold and diligent. And may God be with you as you do your best."

KING JESHOSHAPHAT BEGINS A CHAIN REACTION WITH PRAISE

2 Chronicles 20

The response of Judah's king to the next crisis reflected his strong relationship with God. When scouts reported, "A huge army from three countries is marching against us," the king begged the Lord for guidance. Jeshoshaphat didn't hide his fear, but ordered his people to fast (abstain from food) and pray for three days, then gather in Jerusalem's Temple courtyard to seek God's help.

The king's speech began with an extended prayer of praise. An impatient general might have thought, "Get on with it! We've got weapons and troops to prepare." Delegations from border towns could have muttered, "Ask God for help NOW. The enemy is on our doorstep."

But Jehoshaphat had learned the hard way to focus on the one-and-only God, who had brought them out of slavery in Egypt and adopted them as His people. The king encouraged his countrymen to turn their faces toward God through praise: *"O Lord, God of our ancestors, you alone are the God who is in heaven. You are ruler of all the kingdoms of the earth. You are powerful and mighty; no one can stand against you! ... Your people settled here and built this Temple to honor your name. They said, 'Whenever we are faced with any calamity ..., we can come to stand in your presence before this Temple where your name is honored. We can cry out to you to save us, and you will hear us and rescue us."* (2 Chronicles 20:6-9, NLT). Focused on God, King Jehoshaphat cried out in desperation. "We are powerless against this mighty army. We are coming to You for help."

As the men of Judah stood before the Lord with their wives and children, the Spirit of the Lord spoke through a local man: "Listen, all you people of Judah and Jerusalem! Listen, King Jehoshaphat! This is what the Lord says: Do not be afraid! Don't be discouraged by this mighty army, for the battle is not yours, but God's. Tomorrow, march out against them... But you will not even need to fight. Take your positions; then stand still and watch the Lord's victory. He is with you, O people of Judah and Jerusalem. Do not be afraid or discouraged. Go out against them tomorrow, for the Lord is with you!"

The king and his people bowed low with faces to the ground, worshiping the Lord. Excited and shouting, the clans of Kohath and Korah jumped up to praise their God. Even though their fathers, sons, and brothers would still have to march out to war in a life-or-death struggle, even though they still faced annihilation, God's people began to believe in an impossible victory, and they began jumping, hugging, shouting, and pumping fists in the air. "We're not going to get destroyed! We're going to win!"

As the people praised God, their faith was ignited, and fear faded. They praised God in expectance that God would respond. God declared that He would do the fighting, that the victory was theirs, and they believed Him without knowing the game plan. Their crazy, rambunctious, uninhibited, praise-ignited faith enabled them to march toward the enemy rather than run the other way.

The next day King Jehoshaphat appointed a Levite choir to walk ahead of the troops singing praises: "Give thanks to the Lord; his faithful love endures forever!"

Some of the soldiers following the singers may have grumbled about carrying their weapons in packs on their backs rather than ready in their hands: "How can I fight without a sword in my hand?" "What do you mean, praise is my weapon? That's crazy!"

At the very moment the Levites began to sing and give praise, the Lord caused the three enemy armies to fight among themselves. So, when the army of Judah arrived at the battlefield, the field was covered with dead bodies as far as they could see. Not a single enemy had escaped.

Judah's defeat and total destruction were exchanged for a miracle—and God did the fighting. Instead of dreadful hand-to-hand combat, the Judean army spent three days gathering the enemy's equipment, clothing, and other valuables. Finally, they assembled to praise God in the Valley of Blessing. Then, accompanied by harps, lyres, and trumpets, the army triumphantly proceeded to the Temple of the Lord in Jerusalem, and the thankful celebration continued.

Imagine the testimonies the soldiers may have given to those they had left at home:

> Elias, a shepherd armed with a slingshot, told all who would listen: "Sure I was afraid—I expected to die that day—but I obeyed the king and marched, and when we saw dead bodies everywhere, I was ashamed. I fell to my knees and asked God to forgive me for my doubt."

> Abner, a squad leader in Jehoshaphat's elite guard, couldn't stop talking about how praise had changed everything: "I'm a foot soldier in the front line, so I was right behind the singers. When we left Jerusalem, I was pretty skeptical, but praising God changed us somehow. Soon, we were all marching in rhythm, and our joyful noise was deafening. I don't know what to tell you, we weren't afraid any more. When we got there, the fight was already over. I've never experienced anything like that before."

Back in Jerusalem, crowds filled the streets, gathered at the temple, and the celebration grew pretty rowdy. Jumpin' Jeshoshaphat,* who had led his people in praise, also led them in celebrating their God.

When all the surrounding kingdoms heard that the Lord himself had fought against the enemies of His people, the fear of God came over them. Jehoshaphat's kingdom was at peace, for their God had given them rest on every side.

*Note: While the Bible never refers to Judah's King as "Jumpin' Jehoshaphat," this alliterative phrase was used here to emphasize the king's intense focus on praising God.

WHEN GOD'S ANSWER IS NOT ALL WE ASKED FOR

A Modern-Day True Story of Praise

Acute leukemia threatened Carol, a middle-aged wife and mother of six. While fighting for her life, Carol discovered that she was pregnant. Doctors gave her two choices: receive treatment and most likely lose her baby or delay treatment and face the likely death of both mother and baby. Carol and her husband prayerfully chose to start chemo while the baby was in utero.

A group of prayer warriors regularly interceded for Carol and her unborn child. After meditating, one man told the group that the Holy Spirit had led him to the story of King Jehoshaphat in 2 Chronicles 20, specifically to the word "battle." "We need to pray warfare against this illness," he said. Another was led to the same chapter, but with a focus on "praise." The group's praise became their weapon to battle cancer.

The next week during the hour-and-a-half car ride to the hospital, these warriors praised God and prayed for defeat of Carol's leukemia. At the hospital, they told Carol how God had led them to Jehoshaphat's story and two words: "praise" and "warfare."

Carol—pregnant and bald—immediately knelt next to her hospital bed and led the group in praising God using Psalm 91, which she recited from memory.

Those who live in the shelter of the Most High will find rest in the shadow of the Almighty. This I declare about the Lord: He alone is my refuge, my place of safety; he is my God, and I trust him. For he will rescue you from every trap and protect you from deadly disease. He will cover you with his feathers. He will shelter you with his wings. His faithful promises are your armor and protection... (Psalm 91: 1-4, NLT)

After 33 weeks, Carol gave birth to a beautiful girl they named Faith. Treatment ended, and Carol experienced remission once again. God granted Carol six more years of health. She reveled in her family, shared her faith with everyone she met, and gave her testimony to many.

However, cancer returned once more.

Carol wrote in her journal a few days later: "This was a very hard day. Not yet really believing this could be happening, I had to tell my family. It was hard to open my mouth (can anyone imagine that?) and say the words. So many tears and questions, and yet they all encouraged me in their own beautiful loving ways, reminding me of God's presence, faithfulness, healing power, and past miracles. The next miracle was the powerful, peaceful presence that changed me the next day, as family and friends interceded to the Father, Son, and Holy Spirit on my behalf. Only God could have changed my state of being that quickly and completely. Praise the Lord, to Him be the glory, and honor, and praise!!! Thank you for the prayers. He is alive, and He hears, cares, and answers."

This unwanted news could have devastated Carol and her family, but they knew that God had not abandoned them or was done granting miracles. As Carol testified in her journal: "The next miracle was the powerful, peaceful presence that changed me..." The family praised God for His presence and for bringing them into His family as children and heirs. Even in the face of Carol's impending death, they trusted God to hold and carry them all in His circle of love.

Carol transitioned to her heavenly home a little more than a year later, still praising God, and joined her Lord to live with Him forever. Her family is still dancing in God's Circle of Love on earth as Carol is pirouetting in heaven.

To God be the glory!

Explore and Exercise

1. Even King David, "a man after God's own heart," felt hopeless at times.

   Tears blur my eyes. My body and soul are withering away. I am dying from grief; my years are shortened by sadness. Sin has drained my strength; I am wasting away from within. I am scorned by all my enemies and despised by my neighbors— even my friends are afraid to come near me. When they see me on the street, they run the other way. I am ignored as if I were dead, as if I were a broken pot. I have heard the many rumors about me, and I am surrounded by terror. (Psalm 31:9-13, NLT)

   a. What barriers do you think could be separating David from God based on these verses from Psalm 31? Where is he emotionally?

   David also wrote Psalm 46. Although he is clearly facing trouble again, this time his response is very different.

   God is our refuge and strength, an ever-present help in trouble… You, Lord, are forgiving and good, abounding in love to all who call to you. Hear my prayer, Lord; listen to my cry for mercy. When I am in distress, I call to you, because you answer me. Among the gods there is none like you, Lord; no deeds can compare with yours. All the nations you have made will come and worship before you, Lord; they will bring glory to your name. For you are great and do marvelous deeds; you alone are God. (Psalm 46:1, 5-10, NIV)

   b. Share what you believe made it possible for David to respond so differently in Psalm 46, even though in both instances he was in great danger.

   c. If you have experienced a time of hopelessness, what brought you out of the pit?

2. King David had an affair with the wife of one of his premier soldiers who was away fighting a war for his king. Bathsheba got pregnant, and David let this sin lead him even deeper into the darkness as he tried to cover up his mistake (2 Samuel 11).

God sent the prophet Nathan to confront him, and the result was David flat on his face before the Lord reciting Psalm 51, which he wrote out of his guilt and despair.

David had seen what happened when the Lord withdrew His Holy Spirit from someone—he had watched it happen to King Saul (1 Samuel 16:14). David's sin and disobedience caused him to pull away from his relationship with God; it was a roadblock in their relationship.

    a. In Psalm 51, what did David say about his sin?

    b. In this Psalm, what truths about God did David proclaim?

    c. What did David ask God for?

    d. Discuss the ongoing relationship between David and God, both before and after his affair. What did David proclaim about God in this Psalm, and what changed in him as he did so. How could you use this Psalm as a pathway to forgiveness and faith?

3. **Praise Challenge:** Are you prepared for the temptations, disappointments, sin, pain, and sorrow that are a part of our lives here on earth? Praising God is your preparation and your protection. A panic attack begins, fear paralyzes you, your anger explodes inside you, grief leaves a bitter taste in your mouth, temptation is so strong you can no longer fight it—just say His name: "Jesus." That may be all you can do at first, but repeat his name until you can add, "Thank you, Jesus." In doing so, you are focusing on the Almighty God and the Holy Spirit who lives inside you, and the Holy Spirit holds you up and brings you out of the depths. You don't have to say profound words in a magical cadence or order. You only need to turn to God, and He will bring you through.

4. **Praise Challenge:** Israel's King David journaled his emotional journey that zigzagged through despair to faith and everything in between. Carol and her family also ran through a gamut of feelings during her years of battling cancer. In their

trials, they found that praise was their preferred weapon against the darkness of being cut off from their faith

Praise can also be your weapon of choice against despair. And as is true of all weaponry, we need to keep it oiled and ready to go. We need to practice using it so that when we need a weapon, it is close at hand and feels like a part of us. One way to do this is through music.

- a. Make a song list to play on your preferred devices. Listening can be as easy as: "Alexa, play my praise songs." Start constructing yours today. Bring together songs:
  - i. That celebrate who God is and His grace, mercy, and love for you.
  - ii. That thank Him for carrying you through the hard times.
  - iii. That remind you of how God has cared for you in the past and reveal His promises for right now and the future.
- b. Make listening or singing along with this song list a part of your everyday habits. Share the titles or your playlist with others.

PART 1: CHAPTER 3

What Are You Wearing?

praise

Expressing praise and delight in our Creator helps us to get beyond our little selves and focus on Him, The Great I Am.

God is a relational being. For all eternity, God the Father, Son, and Holy Spirit have been, are, and will be interacting together in what Christians call the Trinity: three-in-one. The Trinity, God in three persons, can also be illustrated as a Circle of Love (see Appendix A: Circle of Love), sharing, and delight. God created us to be in relationship with Him as an outflow of this glorious circle of Trinitarian love. We are invited into this Circle and adopted as God's children so that His love can flow throughout our lives.

All praise to God, the Father of our Lord Jesus Christ, who has blessed us with every spiritual blessing in the heavenly realms because we are united with Christ. Even before he made the world, God loved us and chose us in Christ to be holy and without fault in his eyes. God decided in advance to adopt us into his own family by bringing us to himself through Jesus Christ. This is what he wanted to do, and it gave him great pleasure…The Spirit is God's guarantee that he will give us the inheritance he promised and that he has purchased us to be his own people. He did this so we would praise and glorify him. (Ephesians 1:3-5 & 14, NLT)

In John 14:6, Jesus tells us, *I am the way* (leading us into His Circle of Love), *the truth* (telling us about this Circle), *and the life* (giving us an entry into the Circle). Salvation is more than an insurance policy for eternity, it's an invitation to join God's Circle of Love, to know we are loved, and to live a life expressing God's love.

We express our love for God through PRAISE.

The Westminster Catechism states: "Man's chief end is to glorify God and to enjoy him forever" (1 Corinthian 10:31, Romans 11:36). Pastor and author John Piper suggests a subtle word change in which "enjoy" becomes an active verb in our lives. When we live in the flow of God's Circle of Love, we grow in our ability to express it to others. In relationship with our Father, His love flows through us and grows the love-fruit of the Spirit: joy, peace, patience, kindness, goodness, gentleness, and self-control. And we praise the God who has adopted us (Ephesians 1:5).

We were created to feel, express, and share delight. When we choose to enjoy God, our praise removes fear and the feeling that we need to hide as Adam and Eve did in the Garden of Eden when they sinned (Genesis 3:8). When we focus on God in praise, the Holy Spirit enables us to actively live this way (Psalm 51).

So here's what I want you to do, God helping you: Take your everyday, ordinary life—your sleeping, eating, going-to-work, and walking-around life—and place it before God as an offering. Embracing what God does for you is the best thing you can do for him. Don't become so well-adjusted to your culture that you fit into it without even thinking. Instead, fix your attention on God. You'll be changed from the inside out. Readily recognize what he wants from you, and quickly respond to it. Unlike the culture around you, always dragging you down to its level of immaturity, God brings the best out of you, develops well-formed maturity in you. (Romans 12:1-2, MSG)

DOES PRAISE = WORSHIP?

Worship and praise are woven together so tightly that it is hard to separate them. The differences are subtle. Most importantly, both worship and praise turn our focus to God.

- Praise is **about** God; worship is **to** God.
- Praise is **opening up**; worship is **entering in.**
- Praise is **boldly declaring**; worship is **humbly bowing** in the presence of a Holy God.
- Praise **applauds** what God has done, worship is **honoring God for who He is.**

Worship is about the "worth-ship" of God; it focuses on the value of the Almighty. Praise shows honor to God, gives Him thanks, and celebrates our relationship with him.

Praise is always a part of worship, but worship isn't always praise. These two concepts are so intertwined that you often hear worship flow into praise in the same sentence (as it does in Psalm 19). When we *praise God for what He has done*, it leads us to *worship Him for who He is* and vice versa.

True praise to God is an element of worship, and true worship gives praise to God.

Because these two expressions are a part of the same continuum, when we speak about praise in this book, we include the elements of worship. Praise and worship bring us closer to God (Psalm 138:2).

PRAISE MUST BE EXPRESSED

While God never changes, our praise habits appear in countless styles, as many as can be found in our traditions, situations and individual practices. But whatever praise looks like, it has one thing in common—encouraging others to join in. Think about it. What is your initial response to coming into contact with something or someone wonderful? You invite others to notice and join you in your delight: "Did you see that rainbow?" "Isn't she just the cutest thing you ever saw?" "There's enough power under this hood for anything you might want to do."

In his book *Reflections on the Psalms*, C.S. Lewis makes the argument that praise isn't complete until we add one final component: "expression." Isn't it true that our spontaneous reaction to total enjoyment is to express praise? Lewis goes even further to state that our delight is not complete until it is stated out loud.

BIBLICAL PRAISE

Seven Hebrew words have been translated into English as one word, "praise." Since each Hebrew word contains subtly different meanings of physical, mental, or emotional expressions, we will need to add these distinctions to our praise habits. It might be time to enlarge the closets that hold them.

YADÂH (PRONOUNCED YAW-DAW') means to extend the hand as in the action of shooting an arrow or throwing a stone. In the context of praise, it gives a picture of people so thrilled by God's glory that they throw up their arms (Psalm 28:2).

Picture a crowd at a basketball game. As the guard steals the ball and makes a solo break toward the basket, the fans leap to their feet and throw their hands into the air in excitement. That's what *yadâh* praise looks like.

HÂLAL (PRONOUNCED HAW-LAL') means to boast; to celebrate, or to be enthusiastically foolish.

In our modern era, fans dress up, paint their faces, carry signs, and dance in the stands in celebration of their favorite team or attend conventions dressed in the costumes of their favorite movie or game characters. These passionate fan displays are not usually associated with church services, even though God as Father, Redeemer, and Holy Spirit (residing in you) is the best thing ever (Psalm 149:3)!

Remember King David's crazy celebratory dance when the Ark of the Covenant was returned to Jerusalem (2 Samuel 6). It was as far from dignified, carefully orchestrated worship that would never offend anyone's sensibilities. David's raucous *hâlal* praise pleased God. Could God possibly wish that we, too, would cut loose in unreserved praise?

ZÂMAR (PRONOUNCED ZAW-MAR') means to make music, to celebrate with music and song. As demonstrated in the Book of Psalms (Psalm 57:7), music is associated with worship and praise. In 2 Kings 3, Elisha used music to invite the Lord to prophesy through him, and the music signaled the people, too: "Listen up. You will want to hear and understand these words from God."

> "Next to the Word of God, the noble art of music is the greatest treasure in the world. Beautiful music is the art of the prophets that can calm the agitations of the soul; it is one of the most magnificent and delightful presents God has given us."
>
> ~ Martin Luther

TELHILLAH (PRONOUNCED TEH-HIL-LAW') means a spontaneous or new song of praise. It often adds the nuance of unrehearsed newness, praise that arises from within rather than a scripted recital (Psalm 40:3).

When we praise God with a familiar quote from the Bible such as, *"Our Father Who art in Heaven,"* over time it may become a mere recitation without depth. We can introduce telhillah by digesting and rewriting the words: "You, God, are my good, good father in Heaven who holds my hand as I walk by your side." Or, we might sing a Psalm using a well-known tune—a common practice in the church's history. (For instance, sing Psalm 49 to the tune of "Oh, the Deep, Deep Love of Jesus," Tune: Ebenezer by Williams.) Others could compose an original work to place biblical truths in songs or different styles of music: a choral work, a simple chorus, jazz, or a rhythmic toe-tapper.

The Bible often links prophecy and music. When Samuel anointed Saul to be king, his instructions for Saul began with a combination of music and prophesy (1 Samuel 10:5-7). David selected prophets and musicians to work together (1 Chronicles 25:3). And Paul describes how important it is to *speak* and *sing* with both the mind and the spirit to gain full understanding (Hebrews 4:12). This gift of spontaneous musical praise doesn't come from a vacuum, but flows out of the depths of a person whose mind is filled with the words of God.

> "As we open up our hearts and spirits to sing a spontaneous song unto the Lord, something powerful happens. We move from repeating words that someone else has written to pouring praise from the depths of who we are."
> ~ Mike Redman, Director of Worship & Creative Arts,
> Third Church, Pella, Iowa

SHÂBACH (PRONOUNCED SHAW-BAKH') adds a distinction of tone and volume: to address in a loud tone; to shout; to commend, glory, and triumph.

Think of the roar of a crowd watching the final soccer game of the World Cup. *Shâbach* isn't something we expect to hear in church, but rather in an arena, on a battlefield, or when welcoming a super-star. But our God is the most super of all super-stars—the King of Kings, the great I AM, the Name above Every Name (Psalm 117:1).

TÔWDÂH (PRONOUNCED TO-DAH') means to extend a hand; to give thanksgiving, confession, or a sacrifice of praise; to give thanks for anticipated blessing; it often includes a choir of worshippers.

Have you experienced a service in which the musical praise of the choir or worship band was joined enthusiastically by the congregation? When believers are united together in expectancy and fill the room with praise, faith is ignited and grows from a small flame to a roaring conflagration (Psalm 42:4). God inhabits the praises of his people.

In Psalm 50, Asaph wrote a praise stanza for those who have forgotten God. An act of *tôwdâh* praise may actually be sung before His promises or even salvation occur. Eugene Peterson writes Psalm 50:23 (MSG) this way: *"It's the praising life that honors me. As soon as you set your foot on the Way, I'll show you my salvation."*

BÂRAK (PRONOUNCED BAW-RAK') gives the picture of praising God on our knees: to kneel; to adore; to salute; to thank in a posture of humility. *Bârak* is the proper way to greet a Sovereign King, bending low while keeping your eyes fixed on him. In the humbleness of your station and the acknowledgement of the Ruler of the Universe, you are transfixed on God in reverence, adoration, and thanks (Psalm 72:11, 15).

IT'S ALL ABOUT GOD

We humans egocentrically think our lives are all about us. The truth is, our lives are part of a much bigger drama that is created, written, and directed by God. Madeline L'Engle explored this truth in her poem "Scene III, Act II" (below).

Someone has altered the script.
My lines have been changed.
The other actors are shifting roles.
They don't come on when they're expected to,
and they don't say the line I've written
and I'm being upstaged.
I thought I was writing this play
with a rather nice role for myself,
small, but juicy
and some excellent lines.
But nobody gives me my cues
and the scenery has been replaced
and I don't recognize the new sets.
This isn't the script I was writing.
I don't understand this play at all.
To grow up
is to find
the small part you are playing
in this extraordinary drama
written by
somebody else.
~ Madeleine L'Engle, in *Lines Scribbled on an Envelope and other Poems*, published by Farrar, Strauss, Giroux, 1984

An old Yiddish adage says, "Man plans; God laughs." Our plans for life can be obstructed by scenery, emotions, walls, poor vision, or our own blindness to reality. However, God not only clearly sees each one of us, but He knows us in all space, in all time, in no time, in eternity. Not only does He see us, He created each of us gene by gene and placed us exactly where He wants us to be.

> *Now we see things imperfectly, like puzzling reflections in a mirror, but then we will see everything with perfect clarity. All that I know now is partial and incomplete, but then I will know everything completely, just as God now knows me completely.* (1 Corinthians 13:12, NLT)

The main spiritual actions that God designed in us and for us are praise and delight (Psalm 73:25-26). Expressing our praise and delight in our Creator helps us to get beyond our little selves and to focus on Him, the Great I Am.

God is worthy of all our praise however we offer it: on our knees, with shouting, with music, with the whole church, with our hand lifted high or outstretched in supplication, with hymns, with choirs, or with worship bands.

But express it, we must. It's a part of our DNA. Praise is the habit we wear.

However, it doesn't end there. Praise is a match that ignites the flame of faith and begins a chain reaction of prayer, overcoming evil, and life in the Kingdom of God.

Explore and Exercise

1. We are called to boast about one thing—our magnificent and wondrous God. A great example of boasting about God's saving power is the Jewish Hallel (translated: praise). The Hallel prayers are based on Psalms 113-118 and recited at important Jewish festivals.

   a. Read Psalm 113.

      i. What does this psalm model for us?

      ii. In The Message, verse 2 says: Just to speak his name is praise! Just to remember God is a blessing—now and tomorrow and always. In today's world, His name is spoken more often as an expletive than as praise. How could we use His name in conversation as a form of praise rather than a reaction to shock or pain?

   b. Psalm 114 gives historical background.

      i. Why could history be important for believers?

      ii. If you have personally experienced God-sightings or have seen God's hand at work in orchestrating your life, share your experiences with the class.

   c. The psalmist shifts his attention from the past to the present in Psalm 115.

      i. What reason does the Psalmist give for praise in the first few verses?

      ii. In verses 1-8, the psalmist compares the true God to man-made things that we worship instead. What might the idols be that we worship today? If we made a list of things that are very important to us, how long would that list be? Where is our relationship with God on that list?

      iii. Psalms 116, 117, and 118 weave the previous themes together.

iv. Based on Psalm 116, describe the relationship between God and His people?

v. Enter Psalm 117 in the note section of your phone so you will always carry it with you. When troubles hit and you can't find the words to praise, read this psalm out loud.

vi. Psalm 118 is another over-arching psalm of praise. Memorize verse 1 so that you can repeat it in times of doubt to change your focus and flow your faith.

2. It has been said that God doesn't need our praise and worship; we need it because it transforms us! As we praise God, focusing on the truth of who He is and our relationship to Him, our sense of identity changes.

   a. Why are we called to praise God? What purpose does praise serve for us?

   b. Praise can be expressed in thought, speaking, writing, or singing. In what way or situation do you most often praise God?

3. Name a daily habit that you practice. Is this an acquired mode of behavior (like brushing your teeth) or a personal preference to do things a certain way?

   a. What could be the value and advantages of wearing an identifiable uniform such as a nun's habit or a clerical collar?

   b. Do you think it is important that all "praise habits" look alike or can their styles reflect your personal style preferences, such as classic, preppy, ethnic, chic, or eclectic? Discuss this with the class.

   c. What "habit or uniform" do you wear that is visible to those you interact with? How important is it to you that people know that you believe in and praise God?

4. In the Hebrew language, the Bible includes seven expressions of praise:

- Raised hands (*yadâh*) • Raucously foolish (*hâla*l) • Kneeling in adoration (bârak) • Musical worship and praise, sometimes linked with prophecy (zâmar) Spontaneous, non-scripted praise; often musical (*tehillâh*) • Loud shouting and celebration (*shâbach*) • Thanksgiving, confession, anticipating blessing (*tâwdôh*)

  a. Do any of the Hebrew praise expressions listed above take you out of your comfort zone? Can you identify the root cause of your unease?

  b. Is there a praise expression (see above) that draws you to try it? If you praise God in a way that is not listed above, please share.

  c. Have you ever engaged in crazy, rowdy, dancing cheers at a sporting event? If this kind of activity would make you uncomfortable in a praise and worship during a church service, explain why. How might *hâlal* praise be expressed in your church?

5. Share a time when your life script had an unexpected plot twist and your reaction to it. What difficulties (road blocks) did you meet in your desire to praise? What was the result?

6. **Praise Challenge**: All of us can use reminders during the day to remember the important things—like praising God. Choose a method that fits best for your personality and lifestyle. Here's a few ideas:

  a. Sign up for daily scripture verses on your phone or in your inbox.

  b. Carry a stone in your pocket to signify that "God is my fortress."

  c. Paint his label for you—Beloved, Chosen, Child of the King—on a stone or a shell and put it where you will see it every day.

  d. Print God promises on 3X5 cards and tape them to the inside of your cupboard doors.

e. Use the graphic below (or design your own) as a bookmark.

Chain Reaction of Praise

When we **praise** the Lord in all circumstances

Our **faith** bursts into flame and burns within us,

So that we can **pray** to release God's power and authority

To **overcome evil** in Jesus' name

And **reign and rule with Christ** on earth and in heaven.

PART 1: CHAPTER 4

Let the Praises Begin!

When the Lord is magnified, our problems shrink.

God rescued the Israelites from slavery in Egypt, and His chosen people embarked on what could have been a two-week trip to the Promised Land. However, these former slaves were better at complaining than trusting, so God took them on a 40-year journey through the wilderness—which was in actuality a boot camp of faith instruction. With the Lord as their shepherd, *they received all that they needed* (Psalm 23:1): their shoes and clothing never wore out, they received a daily allotment of food, and when they needed water, God provided. Yet many continued to look at their hardships instead of God, and their faith withered.

Before throwing stones at the obstinate Israelites, we should look to our own hearts. Do we respond with praise when we are sweating in the desert? When we praise Him even in our dry seasons, our faith is activated, and we know that God sends a river of blessings to flow through our lives just as He did for the Israelites.

In the previous chapter we looked at the many facets of praise as it is practiced privately, corporately, musically, verbally, kneeling, dancing, or otherwise. As believers, we not only have something to sing about, but Someone to praise. Let's get started.

WE ARE CALLED TO BE A "PEOPLE OF PRAISE"

God Is Worthy of Our Praise. The Bible gives us many pictures of God, including a rock, a strong fortress, a refuge from danger, the King above all kings, and a warrior. He can command the earth to tremble, the mountains to smoke, and the earth to melt. God is the designer, creator, and ruler of everything.

Not only that, God loves us—the human beings he created. Even though we reject Him time after time, He has made sure that we are still able to have a relationship with Him.

> *You see, at just the right time, when we were still powerless, Christ died for the ungodly. Very rarely will anyone die for a righteous person, though for a good person someone might possibly dare to die. But God demonstrates his own love for us in this: While we were still sinners, Christ died for us.* (Romans 5:6-8, NIV)

Since we first believed, we have been in a relationship with God who never changes.

GOD INHABITS THE PRAISES OF HIS PEOPLE. The Bible states that God is the Lord of Lords and King of Kings. He is supreme in all the universe, but we need to understand this in the light of our sin-corrupted nature. God's original design was for us to walk side-by-side with Him just as Adam and Eve did in the Garden of Eden before they fell for Satan's lies. Once sin entered the world, humanity's focus on God became blurred.

> *For ever since the world was created, people have seen the earth and sky. Through everything God made, they can clearly see his invisible qualities—his eternal power and divine nature. So they have no excuse for not knowing God. Yes, they knew God, but they wouldn't worship him as God or even give him thanks. And they began to think up foolish ideas of what God was like. As a result, their minds became dark and confused. Claiming to be wise, they instead became utter fools.* (Romans 1:20-22. NLT)

We are His people. Psalm 22:3 tells us that God is enthroned in our praise—it is through praise that God's supreme authority in heaven comes down to earth. The Holy Spirit dwells in believers and gives us access to power in the name of Jesus. Praise is a natural byproduct of our relationship with God.

GOD ORDAINED PRAISE AS A WEAPON TO DEFEAT THE ENEMY. Psalm 8:2 tells us that as God's people, we have enemies, but we don't have to be afraid. He has given us a weapon—praise—to defeat our adversaries, and even the weakest and most vulnerable in the Kingdom can wield this weapon!

Chapter 4: Let the Praises Begin

When Jesus lived on earth, He faced temptation in the wilderness when Satan offered to give Him the kingdoms of the world in exchange for a moment of worship. In this way, Satan hoped to establish his authority over Christ, but Jesus told him that praise and worship is reserved only for the One True God.

Praise was the weapon for "Jumpin' Jehoshaphat" and his people when armies threatened them (2 Chronicles 20). Humanly speaking, the Judeans had zero chance of survival, but praise was their weapon, which activated their faith, and God fought the battle for them. Carol's family and prayer partners used praise to battle her cancer, and God gave her a healthy baby and granted six more years of life on earth with her family. In both stories, striking the match of praise ignited faith so that God's followers found hope and joy even while experiencing fear and sorrow.

BECAUSE GOD IS OUR SAFE PLACE. We might hide in bomb shelters or panic rooms. Armed troops could encircle and defend us, but there is no surety of safety in worldly constructs. Isn't it ironic that when we desire security, we keep putting our trust in things that can't really keep us safe? We cling to our armed forces, our job, our possessions, our relationships, our bank accounts, our strength and abilities, our intellect, and our routines. But when circumstances race downhill, all we can do is hang on for dear life. Even though our human security blankets are tangible and might give us a temporary sense of security, they are not a substitute for God. Because things will get worse. When we cry out to God for help, he answers, "I am your life preserver. But in order to be saved, you will have to let go of the sinking ship!"

Jesus gave his disciples a practical lesson on where their safety lies. These skilled fishermen were in the middle of a lake when a violent storm threatened to swamp the boat. When all their efforts were futile, they finally begged Jesus for help, and He calmed the storm. The disciples had to focus on Jesus instead of their own expertise (Matthew 8:23–27). When we *shout to God with joyful praise* even in the most dangerous situations, our faith is ignited, and we remember that *God the Lord Most High is awesome. He is the great King of all the earth* (Psalm 47:1-2).

WE CHANGE INSIDE WHEN WE PRAISE GOD

OUR FOCUS SHIFTS. When we praise God, we acknowledge who is in control—the Ruler and Creator of all things. Instead of wallowing in our weakness, we find the brightness of hope even in the darkest of days. We remember who He is, and we give ourselves into His care. We praise God for who He is for ourselves, and we can also praise on behalf of others who are immobilized by the roadblocks in their relationship with God.

> *God is our refuge and strength, always ready to help in times of trouble. So we will not fear when earthquakes come, and the mountains crumble into the sea...The Lord of Heaven's Armies is here among us; the God of Israel is our fortress. (Psalm 46:1-2, 11, NLT)*

WE ARE THE TEMPLE. In the time of the Persian King Xerxes, entering the king's throne room without permission carried a penalty of death. This law applied to all, even Queen Esther (Esther 5:1-2). What if the throne room of our heavenly King had these rules? If it did, only certain people could pray and only specified topics could be discussed. But God doesn't have office hours or any limits to His time and attention for each and every one of us.

As followers of Christ, our bodies are the temple of God, and the throne room is inside of us (1 Corinthians 6:19-20). The Lord sits on the throne, and Isaiah 6:1 tells us that the train of his robe fills the temple. The throne room is in the temple, and because our bodies are God's temple, our King is always available and eager to converse with His people.

No moment brings greater delight to the King than when his children are in strong relationship with him, involved in everyday conversation, and filled with the Holy Spirit.

WHEN THE LORD IS MAGNIFIED, OUR PROBLEMS SHRINK. The devil tries to make God appear small in our eyes. He endeavors to expand our problems and challenges until they seem insurmountable. He wants to break our fellowship with God—which is what he did in the Garden of Eden with his insinuations and lies to Adam and Eve about the "truth" of the fruit of a certain tree that God had forbidden them to eat. They focused on Satan's lies

Chapter 4: Let the Praises Begin

rather than God's words, and for the moment, they lost connection to their faith.

When the sun is behind us, our shadows are bigger than we are. On the other hand, when we turn our face toward the sun, we can feel its warmth and strength, and now our shadows are behind us. Our eyes are fixed on God, not on our problems. Go outside and try it: face the sun, feel its warmth on your face, and notice that the shadows are behind you.

This is what happens when we praise God—our focus and emotions are redirected. We remember who God is: all-powerful and all-loving. When our faces are turned toward Him, the shadows' importance shrinks. We bask in His love, cling to Him in trust, our faith is ignited, and we are surrounded by the peace that this holy fire brings. He holds our future in His hands.

WE LEARN TO DESIRE THAT WHICH REALLY FILLS US. When we reach a certain age and look back over our lives, we often realize that everything we desired in our twenties, thirties, and beyond is either in the junkyard rusting, decaying in a landfill, or deteriorating with age. It is common to realize that our desires shift every five to seven years because we can't really settle on what it is that we truly desire.

Praising God feeds our spirits, quenches our thirst, and draws us into God's abundance instead of human scarcity. The more we learn, the more we desire the things of God, and our capacity to be filled with more of God keeps expanding as we continue to walk with Him. It is in desiring the truths of God's Kingdom that we find fulfillment.

After Jesus was crucified, was buried, and had disappeared from the tomb, two of his followers left Jerusalem for their home in Emmaus. As they walked, struggling to sort out all that had happened in the last three days, a man joined them, and they found themselves sharing all their disappointment, fear, and confusion with Him. This stranger then took them through the scriptures, which they thought they knew already, and pointed out the prophecies that had foretold the events of the last few weeks.

The friends wanted to hear more of what this mysterious stranger had to say, so they begged him to spend the night with them in Emmaus. At supper, as their guest broke the bread and blessed it, they suddenly realized who he was, and then He disappeared.

> *"Why didn't we recognize it was him? Didn't our hearts burn with the flames of holy passion while we walked beside him? He unveiled for us such profound revelation from the Scriptures!"* (Luke 24:32, TPT)

Within an hour these two Jesus followers were hurrying back to Jerusalem to tell the disciples what had happened. While they were all together, Jesus appeared in the middle of the group.

Jesus opened their minds and hearts to understand the things of God (Luke 24:45). As they walked and talked, they moved beyond memorization into a fuller understanding of God's word and experienced free-flowing conversation with God. Isn't that what we also desire? It's a desire that we won't outgrow as the years pass. The more we listen to God's words, the more His truth is revealed to us, the more we experience an intimate relationship with Him (Hebrews 12:4).

OUR HEARTS TURN TO THANKSGIVING AND GRATITUDE. All of us have a desire to praise and worship something; it is how we were created. By default, our souls will praise, be it a graven image, a philosophy, riches, science, or another human being. Could it be that we are our own idols?

In their book, *The Way Back*, authors Phil Cooke and Jonathan Bock challenge us to consider the God we worship.

How much do your wants and demands determine your relationship with God? Do you approach the Creator of the universe on His terms or yours? What commandments, verses, and instructions do you consider to be no longer relevant to your contemporary lifestyle? Have you conformed your worldview to God's, or have your ideas of who you think God should be modified His worldview to conform to yours?
~ Phil Cooke and Jonathan Bock, *The Way Back*,
Worthy Publishing, Franklin, TN, pg 42

Chapter 4: Let the Praises Begin

Praise God, the Bible tells us, even if, and especially when, you have had your worst day ever.

As you examine your spiritual journey, you will find evidence that God was with you then and is with you now. God has carried you in His arms when you couldn't go on, and His promise is to always carry you then, now, and in the future. Praise God, and your hearts will fill with thankfulness and gratitude.

PRAISING GOD IS AN ACT OF WILL, NOT A RESPONSE TO CIRCUMSTANCES

- If you are lying in the mud at the bottom of a foxhole with bombs bursting all around,
  bullets flying, and there is no escape,
  strike the match—choose to focus on God with praise.

- When you want so much to have a child,
  but the proof that you are not pregnant appears
  month after month, year after year,
  strike the match—choose to focus on God with praise.

- If your business goes belly-up,
  and you don't have the money to feed your family,
  strike the match—choose to focus on God with praise.

- If your spouse leaves, your child wanders from the faith,
  or the fighting among your siblings causes pain,
  strike the match—choose to focus on God with praise.

- When cancer ravages your body,
  and God doesn't give you a miracle cure,
  strike the match—choose to focus on God with praise.

God didn't create robots. He made human beings in his own image, and that included our ability to choose—what we will wear, eat, say, think, do, and worship. When we decide to strike the match of praise, our faith bursts into flame, and our God becomes a safe refuge, the source of all hope, the great physician, the light of the world, the alpha and omega, the good shepherd, and the Savior who carries us to victory.

Even when I walk through the darkest valley, I will not be afraid, for you are close beside me. Your rod and your staff protect and comfort me. (Psalm 23:4, NLT)

Choosing to wear a habit of praise despite any circumstances requires an act of your will. So go to your closet to choose what you will wear today—your praise habit—and develop an iron will for the things of God no matter what. The habit you choose to wear turns your focus away from the problem and toward the Ruler of heaven and earth.

God has laid out the fire of faith inside you. Strike the match, light the fire.

In Acts 16, Paul and Silas were beaten and bleeding, immobilized in stocks, and well-guarded in a dank, dirty dungeon. What did they do? Paul and Silas chose to praise God. They could do so because praising God was the daily habit they wore. And God's response was amazing.

Like Paul and Silas, we can be heroes of faith if we daily focus on God through praise. That is how we are renewed, sanctified, transformed into people who walk in faith (Romans 12:2), so that even in the darkest of times we have access to the flames inside us. That's what heroes do: strike the match of praise, and ignite the fire of faith.

Let the praises begin!

Praise God from whom all blessings flow;
Praise Him all creatures here below;
Praise Him above ye heavenly hosts;
Praise Father, Son, and Holy Ghost.

Explore and Exercise

1. In Medieval times, safety was pictured as a castle surrounded by a moat. During the Cold War era, it may have been a well-stocked bomb shelter buried deep in your backyard. Today, our safety entails satellites, drones, and smart bombs. Identify and describe an earthly haven that may make you feel secure.

2. "Ascending into God's Heavenly Throne Room" is a phrase that Christians use to express having open access to conversation with God. A human equivalent to this might be the opportunity to peek in the door of the Oval Office in the White House any time day or night: to come in, make yourself comfortable, and chat with the President about whatever is on your mind. With God, you don't have to try to secure an empty slot in a crowded calendar, pass through any security checks, or meet any qualifications. God has given us a "Get in Free" card.

    a. What does our free access to the throne room tell us about our relationship with God?

    b. If you were invited to consult with the CEO of Google every day, would you take advantage of it? Why or why not? Is God's invitation any less important?

    c. What do we acknowledge when we praise God? Why do you think praise could be considered our access key to the throne room?

    d. **Personal Challenge**: If you met face-to-face with God today, what would you like to talk about?

3. Psalm 8 describes praise as a weapon that can be used by anyone.

    Lord, your name is so great and powerful!
    People everywhere see your splendor.
    Your glorious majesty streams from the heavens,
    filling the earth with the fame of your name!
    You have built a stronghold by the songs of babies.

Strength rises up with the chorus of singing children.
This kind of praise has the power to shut Satan's mouth.
Childlike worship will silence the madness of those who oppose you.
(Psalm 8:1-2, TPT)

    a. Psalm 22:3 tells us that *God inhabits our praises*. Based on these verses, what do you think it is about praise that makes it a weapon that can overcome evil?

    b. Imagine a situation (or role play it in class) in which you are threatened by an evil protagonist, and you choose to praise God in response.

    c. How is evil thwarted in your scenario?

    d. If you have been harmed, how has praise been an effective weapon?

4. Romans 1 gives us a picture of people who have chosen to live without God—people in rebellion. We call them atheists: "a theist" which is Latin for "without God."

Consider the contrast between theoretical atheism (a belief that there is no God) and practical atheism (one lives however one desires). Practical atheism is visible in those who may profess God with their own lips, but their professed belief does not affect the way they live their lives.

    a. Discuss what this kind of atheism might look like in your life, your church, or your family today.

    b. Could the habit of praise and practical atheism co-exist? Is this only a personal issue or does it apply to a community also?

5. Share habits of praise that you have begun wearing in your daily life. What difference has praise made in the relationship between you and God?

6. Praise Challenge: Choose a text that brings you to a focus on God and why He is worthy of praise.

a. Memorize the text that you chose or print it up and place where you will see it multiple times a day. Say it (preferably out loud) throughout every day.

b. Use your search engine to find a praise text illustrated in a way that speaks to you. Use it as the home screen on your devices.

c. Make your own "praise doodle" based on your praise text of choice. Artistic excellence is not a criterion here, but draw something that turns your focus to God. For example, below is a sketch that I, Kathleen, made as I read Colossians 2:9.

PART 2

Faith

Faith is a God-given fire
that burns inside each one of us.

Caught without shelter in a storm, you struggle to light a fire. The wind blows the match out, and the kindling is wet. You need the fire for warmth, food, or perhaps even to save your life, but no matter how hard you try, you aren't able to light a fire.

When spiritual storms blow into our lives, our desperate efforts to save ourselves can also seem futile. But what would it be like if faith was our default reaction to threats? Good news!

We will all experience storms, and even when we feel helpless and hopeless, we have access to the faith that God has given us. It may be beyond our strength, but not God's. The Holy Spirit tells us, "Don't be afraid. I have provided clear instructions—a never-fail safety kit—to spark the fire of faith that I have given you."

Praise is the match that can't be blown out, and its tiny spark ignites our praise. When we turn our faces toward God and praise Him, even storm-dampened kindling ignites, and soon we are warming ourselves by faith's fire.

> *For it is by grace you have been saved, through faith—and this not from yourselves, it is the gift of God—not by works, so that no one can boast. For we are God's workmanship, created in Christ to do good works, which God prepared in advance for us to do.* (Ephesians 2:8-9, NIV)

You might ask, "Will my faith be enough?" Try it and see. God has laid the fire faith inside you, ready for you to strike the match of praise and watch it burst into flame. Warmed by the fires of God-given faith, the chain reaction continues so that you will be able to pray for God's power to overcome evil, and live in the Kingdom of God here on earth and forever in heaven.

PART 2: CHAPTER 5

Story Time: Past and Present

"I was contagious—not with a virus, but with praise."

GIDEON: FROM FLEECE TO FAITH

An Old Testament Story of Faith, Judges 6-7

Who was Gideon? He was a frightened man threshing wheat in a winepress to hide from the Midianites. The Angel of God greeted him, "The Lord is with you, mighty warrior." Startled, Gideon ignored the "mighty warrior" designation and whined in the winepress. "If the Lord is with us, why is all this bad stuff happening? Where are all His wonders that our ancestors told us about?"

The Lord ignored Gideon's complaint, and said, "Go in the strength you have and save Israel out of Midian's hand. Am I not sending you?"

"In the strength I have? I think you have the wrong guy!" Gideon protested. "My clan is the weakest one in the area, and I'm no hero."

"I will be with you, and you will strike down all the Midianites, leaving none alive," the Lord told him.

Gideon tried again to avoid this assignment. "Sorry, sir, but I need you to prove to me who you really are first. I'll prepare an offering for you. Don't go away, please."

The Lord waited under an oak tree while Gideon killed and cooked a young goat and baked unleavened bread. When he placed the food on a rock and poured broth over it, fire flared from the angel's staff until all the food was gone. Then the angel of the Lord disappeared.

Gideon trembled with fear until the Lord's voice assured him, "Peace! Do not be afraid. You are not going to die."

Assured, Gideon built an altar there and praised God. Afterward the Lord told him, "Tear down your father's altar to Baal and its accompanying Asherah pole and replace it with an altar to me." Old patterns are hard to break, and while Gideon did what God asked, he waited until night to cover his actions with darkness. When the townspeople discovered his deed and gathered to demand punishment, Gideon once again hid, this time behind his father who faced down the hostile crowd.

How fearful was Gideon the next time God came calling? An army of 135,000 soldiers set up camp nearby preparing to make war on Israel. The Spirit of the Lord came on Gideon, so he blew a battle call on his trumpet. As recruits gathered, fear barricaded Gideon from his faith in God. Again, he asked God for evidence of His presence, not just once, but twice:

> *Then Gideon said to God, "If you are truly going to use me to rescue Israel as you promised, prove it to me in this way. I will put a wool fleece on the threshing floor tonight. If the fleece is wet with dew in the morning but the ground is dry, then I will know that you are going to help me rescue Israel as you promised." And that is just what happened. When Gideon got up early the next morning, he squeezed the fleece and wrung out a whole bowlful of water.* (Judges 6:36-38, NLT)

The next night Gideon asked to wake up to a dry fleece surrounded by dew-covered ground. Once again God supplied the proof Gideon needed.

Gideon's volunteer army of 32,000 men set up camp just south of the enemy. The Lord knew that such a large army would cause the Israelites to brag that victory was won in their own power, so He instructed Gideon to send away those who were afraid. Relieved, 22,000 men hurried toward home.

Now the odds were four enemies to one Israelite, but God ordered yet another reduction by watching the men drink from the spring. Most of the 10,000 remaining soldiers got down on their knees to drink, while only 300 men cupped water in their hands and lapped the water with their tongues.

The Lord told Gideon, "Keep only the 300 lappers with you. I will save you with this tiny army and give the Midianites into your hands." So, Gideon dismissed 9,700 more fighters who went home, leaving their provisions and trumpets for the remaining 300 soldiers.

Who was Gideon when the odds were 450 to 1? Very afraid, but God didn't tell him to "man up." Instead, the Lord repeated His promise of victory and, unasked, offered another sign. To receive it, Gideon and his servant had to sneak down to the enemy camp—a dangerous excursion. In spite of his terror, Gideon obeyed God.

Trembling in the shadows of enemy tents, the two Israelites heard an enemy soldier talking about his terrifying dream: "A round loaf of barley bread came tumbling into our camp and struck the tent with such force that it collapsed."

"Barley bread is poor man's food," responded his companion. "The bread must be Gideon, son of Joash, the Israelite—he's as poor as they come. I think your dream means that God has given the Midianites and our whole camp into his hands."

Who was Gideon when he heard this conversation? God had brought this fearful man to just the right spot to overhear the prophetic dream of an enemy soldier and its interpretation. Gideon bowed down immediately and silently praised God, and as he did, he felt the full heat of his flaming faith.

Gideon returned to camp fully focused on God and the promised victory so that he could be the "mighty warrior" God desired—not in the power of his own bravery, but filled to overflowing with faith in God's power. He told his remnant army of 300 to follow his lead. "Watch me, and do exactly what I do. When I blow my trumpet, then from all around the camp blow yours and shout, 'For the Lord and for Gideon.'"

The tiny army fought the battle by praising God with a loud shout, a form of praise known in Hebrew as shâbach. God did the rest.

Gideon and his men shouted their praise to God, and their faith ignited and roared into life. And God gave them the victory in a way they could never imagine, against 450 to 1 odds.

It was not their strength, but God's.

They did not rely on their own prowess or power, but instead acted in faith-filled confidence that somehow God would bring the victory He had promised.

FAITH DISPLACES FEAR

A Modern-day True Story of Praise Igniting Faith

Sometimes life can be made up of too-short interludes between crises and hospitalizations. During one of those times, two-month-old Carrie was in the hospital again, and the overflowing pediatric ward was understaffed. I asked the nurse to check on my baby, but she expressed no cause for concern.

I had to abandon polite requests and insist that they call the doctor. As I waited anxiously for her arrival, I could see my baby's life slipping away. I knelt by her bed and rubbed her cheeks and sang to her: all four verses of Amazing Grace, over and over again. And as I sang, something changed in me and in that room—terror lost its foothold.

I stopped singing as the doctor examined her, and Carrie stopped breathing. "Code blue!" Staff came running with a crash cart, and I got chased from the room just as my husband arrived. We held each other in the waiting room—not knowing, afraid, in tears—until I started humming Amazing Grace in between sobs. And the room's atmosphere changed once again. We told each other,

"It's okay. Either we'll be holding her in our arms or Jesus will be hugging her close." When the doctor finally stepped into the room, she expressed surprise at our composure. We told her it wasn't our strength; it was God's peace.

At that time, I didn't connect the dots—that it was praise that had activated our faith—but that is exactly what we had experienced.

Fast forward about 30 years: our miracle-baby daughter gave birth to her second child after a difficult pregnancy. At six weeks of age, Oren was hospitalized for pneumonia. I was ill with a virus and couldn't go to the hospital, but Sunday morning I made it out of bed and to church. Our pastor introduced the chain reaction of praise and quoted this scripture:

> *Always be joyful. Never stop praying. Be thankful IN all circumstances, for this is God's will for you who belong to Christ Jesus. Do not stifle the Holy Spirit.* (1 Thessalonians 5:16-18, NLT)

I arrived home to a message from my daughter, "Mom, please come. He's getting worse." I packed a bag and headed to Waterloo.

I felt myself losing emotional control as I drove, so I took some deep breaths and tried to focus on the message that I had just heard: "Praise God IN all circumstances." I couldn't form words of praise in my mind, much less make them come out of my mouth, so I tried listening to Christian radio. Still, nothing penetrated my anxiousness. Finally, the Holy Spirit prompted a song from my memory banks, The Doxology, and as I sang these words of praise in my car, the kindling of faith burst into flame. My voice grew hoarse from singing as the heat from this faith fire produced more fuel that fed my faith: "Praise God from whom all blessings flow. Praise him all creatures here below. Praise him above, ye heavenly host. Praise Father, Son, and Holy Ghost. Amen."

Believe me, I didn't feel like any blessings were flowing in my life just then, but I had heard God's word for me that morning—"Praise Me no matter what!"—so I sang. And something changed in me, in my heart, in my car. As I sang the memorized words of praise over and over, I began to remember and believe God's promises and trust in His love. The peace God gave me as I drove accompanied me into that baby's hospital room, and I shared it with the distressed parents of this tiny boy. And once again the Holy Spirit filled a hospital room with faith, trust, and peace.

I cradled that little baby—oxygen tubes, IV, and all—and for hours "The Doxology" was his lullaby. That song still fills my mind when I snuggle with this lively eight-year-old boy.

I was contagious—not with a virus, but with praise.

It was my choice to praise God that ignited my faith and sparked that of my family, so that we could experience God's peace even in a hospital room.

Explore and Exercise

1. How did the Angel of the Lord respond to Gideon's fear throughout this story? What effect did God's responses have on Gideon?

2. Gideon was by nature a cautious man; some might say timid (Judges 6). God knew that, yet Gideon was the one He chose to tear down idols and to lead an army against the Midianites. Later (Judges 7), Gideon raised a large army to fight the enemy; however, God whittled his fighting force down to a mere 300 soldiers.

   a. Discuss possible purposes for God's choices of: (1) Gideon as leader, and (2) allowing only 300 soldiers to go into battle.

   b. As you read this story, what do you learn about God in His relationship with Gideon? What does that tell you about His relationship with us?

3. Do you have a memory of receiving God-given peace or direction in a troubled moment? As you remember this time, can you identify how you felt before God's intervention? How did this compare to what came next?

4. Worship Director Mike Redman states, "The person with the most hope in the room controls the environment." That was the grandmother's experience when she joined the parents in her grandson's hospital room.

   a. Imagine a mixed group of believers and unbelievers in a tense or dangerous situation. How could a hope-filled Christian change the atmosphere?

   b. Would it be effective to stand up and give your testimony in the middle of the tension? Or are there other ways you can express your hope in a way that is contagious? Explain.

5. **Faith Challenge**. Both of today's stories showed what a difference being filled with faith makes in our lives:

Gideon was given repeated reassurance from God, which changed his focus from his fear to God, accessing his faith and enabling him to step into the action that God called him to do.

In the case of both babies, mother/grandmother knew God was in control, but needed help to choose to praise God in order to reach and hold onto her faith.

a. If a storm hits today, what kind of practice, visual, object, phrase, music, or electronic reminder will you choose to use to focus on God instead of the wind and rain? What habits have you developed to stay in close relationship with your Lord and Savior?

b. Share a time in which you asked God for confirmation or proof of His prompting in your life.

c. Do you pay attention to God's hand in your life every day? Watch for Him and keep a list of God-sightings as a part of your daily devotions or share these moments during family meals or when gathering with friends.

PART 2: CHAPTER 6

Faith, God's Gift of Grace

Faith's fire provides our only comfort in life and death—a gift from our God with whom we have a deep-seated relationship.

FAITH IS NOT ABOUT US; IT'S ABOUT GOD

Some have nicknamed the 20th century "The Age of Anxiety" as evidenced by its bomb shelters, big armies, nuclear bombs, drugs, booze, abortion, euthanasia, and every brand of escapism imaginable. Suggested nicknames for the 21st century include: "The Oh-Oh Decades," "The Great Regression," and "The Blunder Years." We've put our faith in humanism, political structures, fate, Scientology, money, power—all kinds of world-based ideologies. And we're still anxious.

Benjamin Franklin is credited with saying, "In this world nothing can be said to be certain, except death and taxes." John F. Kennedy declared, "The one unchangeable certainty is that nothing is unchangeable or certain." Even the way we use the word "faith" has a diminished meaning. We might say, "I have faith in you," to spur a listener to action, but our crossed fingers show that our faith is wishful thinking rather than trust.

We can't count on anything! Except we can. As Christ-followers, we don't have to cross our fingers. Faith has nothing to do with how great people are, because people aren't. The validity of our faith comes from the God in whom it is placed. In faith we can see the invisible, believe the implausible, and receive the impossible.

> *The fundamental fact of existence is that this trust in God, this faith, is the firm foundation under everything that makes life worth living. It's our handle on what we can't see. The act of faith is what distinguished our ancestors, set them above the crowd. By faith, we see the world called into existence by God's word, what we see created by what we don't see.* (Hebrews 11:1-3, MSG)

The Heidelberg Catechism is a Biblically-supported, personalized declaration of faith. Written in 1563 and still used in churches to this day, it begins with this question and answer:

Q. What is your only comfort in life and in death?

A. That I am not my own, but belong—body and soul, in life and in death—to my faithful Savior, Jesus Christ.

He has fully paid for all my sins with his precious blood, and has set me free from the tyranny of the devil. He also watches over me in such a way that not a hair can fall from my head without the will of my Father in heaven; in fact, all things must work together for my salvation.

Because I belong to him, Christ, by his Holy Spirit, assures me of eternal life and makes me wholeheartedly willing and ready from now on to live for him.

What is faith? The Bible tells us that faith is a complete trust that is based on our knowledge of who God is and that He is worthy of that trust. It is our confidence in Jesus Christ and in His power, so that even when things don't follow our plans, we remain confident in God because of who He is.

Faith is the fire that provides our only comfort in life and death—a gift to us from our God with whom we have a deep-seated relationship. Our trust is not a wish or a vague hope that He loves and cares for us, but a firm knowledge that The Great I Am who was, is, and always will be loves us and has adopted us as His children and heirs.

Because God desires a relationship with us, He has provided a weapon even the smallest and weakest of us can wield against fear (Psalm 8:2). Praise is that weapon: the match that lights the flames of faith. God has also given us a helper—The Holy Spirit—so that we can live in proximity to this blazing fire (Luke 24:49). And faith prompts us, like Peter, to step out the boat, trusting that God will pull us out of the water (Matthew 14).

Life in this world without God is empty, and it is hell in eternity.

WE CAN'T GRAB HOLD OF FAITH
BY TRYING HARDER

Romans 12:3 tells us that each one of us is provided a measure of faith, and it's just the amount we need. Our faith—whole-hearted trust—is a gift of sheer grace that God gave to us out of His deep, deep love. We live in union, in identification, with Christ (Galatians 2:20).

When situations throw us into wrestling matches of doubt versus faith, we often try harder to believe, but our best efforts get us nowhere. Why doesn't it work? Because our own strength is NOT enough: not now, not ever. Like Gideon, we need to change our focus from our weakness to our Almighty God. The better you get to know God, the more capacity you will have to hold His fullness.

Even Jesus' twelve disciples struggled with faith at times. In Mark 9, a father brought his demon-possessed son to the disciples, and they gave it their best shot—they tried and tried—but they were unable to drive the evil spirit out of the boy.

> After that failure, the desperate father appealed to Jesus. *"But if you can do anything, take pity on us and help us."*
>
> *"'IF you can?" Jesus asked. "Everything is possible for one who believes."*
>
> *Immediately the boy's father exclaimed, "I do believe; help me overcome my unbelief!"*

The disciples had tried to overcome evil, but they hadn't yet understood how to fully trust in the invisible, impossible, miraculous power of Jesus Christ. Instead, they tried harder in their own power. Jesus told the boy's father to believe, and this fear-filled man needed Jesus' help to do even that—to thrive in faith rather than strive in our own power. So did the disciples. So do we. We need to change our focus, put it fully on God, not on whatever storm we are caught up in.

Listen up, followers of Jesus! This is a spiritual battle. The devil loves to plant doubts in our minds that, "we don't believe enough" or that "our faith is insufficient." He wants us to be desperate and uncertain, but God tells us the same thing He told Gideon, "Don't be afraid." The Angel of God didn't tell Gideon to try harder, but gave him a sign that changed his focus from his own puny efforts to God's ultimate strength. Faith is following God's prompt to creep into the enemy's camp and receive God's assurance that victory is assured.

In this world, we will all experience trials. Like Gideon we may figure out pretty quickly that our strength won't get us very far. But we, too, can strike a match that the world's storms can't blow out. **Our choice to praise God changes our focus and ignites the blazing fire of faith that God has placed inside each of us. We are called to live in His fullness, not our own.** In faith, we can pray for God's power to overcome evil.

IT'S YOUR CHOICE

God created humankind with the ability to choose: good or evil, right or wrong, self or others, God or Mammon. We were designed to live in eternal loving fellowship with God the Father, Son, and Holy Spirit, sharing a love that is not coerced or mandated.

What if we could choose a natural physical need that supplied life, such as a beating heart, drawing a deep breath into our lungs, or food? All are requirements for life, not daily rituals we can choose or ignore. We treasure food when we've gone without; we cherish oxygen when we experience the lack of it. We were created by God with daily physical needs. The same is true of our spiritual lives. Praise is life-giving, and, as such, a necessary daily habit.

> *They were also to stand every morning to thank and praise the Lord. They were to do the same in the evening.* (1 Chronicles 23:30, NIV)

"Praise God each morning and evening" was on the task list King David assigned to the Levites, who were called to faithfully serve the people of God. God created humankind for fellowship and loving relationship with Him, an echo of the loving interaction

Chapter 6: Faith: God's Gift of Grace

of one God in three persons—the Trinity. David instructed the spiritual leaders of the Israelites to express their love for God with praise—and in doing so, their faith was activated.

In Jesus' day, Pharisees knew that praise was a weapon that the Jesus-followers used against them. They hated that people praised Jesus and insisted He make them stop. He refused their demand because praise is a necessary ritual of the world He created.

"If they kept quiet, the stones would do it for them, shouting praise." (Luke 19:40, MSG)

Praise is a weapon that we, too, can choose to wield—so strike the match that lights the fire of our faith inside us. The devil hates it when we praise God.

Like oxygen and a pulse, like food and drink, a relationship with God is not something to take for granted, but an essential, habitual part of living. When life is good, do we spend time in relationship with God or do we leave our faith simply recessed in the overhead compartment, like an oxygen mask in an airplane, for use in emergencies? If praising God is not part of our everyday habits, our faith may fall out of reach when circumstances threaten us so much that God is our only comfort. This is as true for us as it was for many well-known characters in the Bible; David is a good example.

Once he was anointed by Samuel to be Israel's king, David spent years transitioning from shepherd boy to king. Between his anointing and the long-awaited actualization of God's purpose in his life, David was often on the run. Many of his psalms were written out of despair, and these songs give us a peek into his diary.

In Psalm 18, David was discouraged, alone, and tired of waiting for God's promise to become his reality. This song swings back and forth on an emotional pendulum, from feeling desperately apart from God to the confidence of who he was in God.

David chose to begin with praise: *"you are my rock, my fortress, my deliverer, and my strength,"* and declared his trust that God was all these things for him even though he had to hide to survive. This is significant. In a desperate situation, David used praise as a weapon against his own fear and despair. He declared to himself and to any listeners, "I will not be afraid, for I have faith that the Lord is with me." David sang words of praise to convince himself to let go of fear, to live in God's purpose, and to remember that God held him in His hands.

This weapon works for us as well. Whether we are inwardly depending on our own strength or outwardly overwhelmed by circumstances, when we choose to praise the Almighty God who can never be separated from us, our focus changes (Romans 8:38-39). Just as it did for David, we move from despair to hope. Believe it! Praise is the ultimate weapon that even the weakest and most timid can use to ignite the faith they have been given.

In Psalm 18:3, David celebrated victory even though he no idea of how or when God's promises would be fulfilled. Instead of praying to be king now, tomorrow, or next month at the latest—a timeline this young man probably preferred—David trusted that something good would come from God in His timing. David knew that *faith is confidence in what we hope for and assurance about what we do not see* (Hebrews 11:3, NIV).

The rest of Psalm 18 shows us that David is still battling his emotions. He used poetic language in verses 4 to 15 to describe his danger and added a desperate cry for help. However, by verse 16, he once again drew his weapon and spoke in amazement about God's response, *"He reached down from on high and took hold of me; he drew me out of deep waters."*

When David chose to praise God, he connected with his faith. His confidence didn't come out of his own skills and strength, but by remembering who he was in God. *"You, Lord, keep my lamp burning; my God turns my darkness into light. With your help I can advance against a troop; with my God I can scale a wall"* (verses 28-29). He continues with a long list of all the things that *"God in him"* made possible. By verse 35, David declared, *"Your help has made me great."*

Throughout his psalm diary, after David admitted his fear, he would often say, "but then I entered the sanctuary." He used praise to get access to this place of refuge that filled him with peace, hope, and love—abiding faith in Almighty God. That sanctuary is there for us, too.

The Great I AM, the one from whom all faith originates, loves us, redeems us, and adopts us as His children and heirs. If we are in Christ, and Christ is in us, all of our circumstances are in God's hands. As pastor, speaker, and author, Graham Cooke likes to say, "When you feel overwhelmed by your circumstances, remember that your circumstances are overwhelmed by God."

- When darkness surrounds you,
  strike the match; it only takes a spark.

- When temptations overwhelm you,
  enter the sanctuary with praise and access your faith.

When we develop the habit of praising God in any and all of the circumstances or emotions we experience, this tiny spark ignites a Holy Spirit fire of faith. And the chain reaction continues, each action triggering the next, so that we move forward into purposeful lives of faith, praying for God's power to overcome evil as members of the Kingdom of God.

Explore and Exercise

1. Re-read Heidelberg Catechism Q & A #1 (below). Review the texts from which these statements of faith were drawn.

   Q. What is your only comfort in life and in death?

   A. That I am not my own (1 Cor 6:19-20), but belong—body and soul, in life and in death (Romans 14:7-9)—to my faithful Savior, Jesus Christ (1 Cor 3:23; Tit 2:14).

   He has fully paid for all my sins with his precious blood (1 Pet 1:18-19; 1 Jn 1:7, 2:2),

   and has set me free from the tyranny of the devil (Jn 8:34-36; Heb 2:14; 1 Jn 3:8).

   He also watches over me in such a way (Jn 6:39-40, 10:27-30; 2 Thess 3:3; 1 Pet 1:5) that not a hair can fall from my head without the will of my Father in heaven (Mt 10:29-31; Lk 1:16-18); in fact, all things must work together for my salvation (Rom 8:28).

   Because I belong to him, Christ, by his Holy Spirit, assures me of eternal life (Rom 8:15-16; 2 Cor 1:21-22, 5:5; Eph 1:13-14) and makes me wholeheartedly willing and ready from now on to live for him (Romans 8:14).

   Based on the (scripture-based) answer above:

   a. What do you receive from God the Father? From Jesus Christ? From the Holy Spirit?

   b. How does this give you comfort in this life? For Eternity?

2. Do you know what you will say if a non-believer asks you to explain what faith is? How will you describe what faith means to you?

   a. How is faith in God different than faith in another person, no matter their station or position of power?

   b. What part does trust play in faith?

Chapter 6: Faith: God's Gift of Grace

3. If you ask a search engine, "What is the purpose of faith in God?" you will find an answer similar to this: "The purpose of faith is to act as a measure of a person's hope and to help a person grow in his or her trust in God the Father and in God's purposes for us as his children."
   a. How does faith influence our ability to have hope? To love? To obey?
   b. What roadblocks or walls might you have within you that could hinder your access to faith and obedience?
4. In Psalm 18, David talked about being entangled in the cords of death, being overwhelmed with torrents of destruction, and being so distressed that his only possible action was to cry, "HELP!"
   a. What kind of circumstances have required you to make a conscious effort to choose faith over something that might have seemed a more logical response?
   b. David started the psalm with a declaration of who God is, and that reality then seemed to slip out of his grasp for a while. What do you think happened between verses 1-2 and 3-6?
   c. Using Psalm 18, show how David fought his way back to faith, hope, and peace. Why do you think he could so effectively wield this weapon?
5. **Faith Challenge**: Not all of us have been called to face a huge army with only 300 soldiers as Gideon was or to hide from a king who was out to kill us. Compared to that, our daily faith challenges may seem pretty minor. But remember that this battle wasn't the first thing that God asked of Gideon in which he had to act in faith. God first gave him opportunities to practice his faith in less deadly situations.

   Pick one of the situations below or use one from your own life or imagination. How might a praise-habit-to-access-faith affect your responses?

a. You've had a disagreement with a coworker or family member. You're frustrated and feel like lashing out in anger.

b. You've been blessed to have a good friend live nearby, and now they've decided to move away. You've always done everything together. Now what?

c. You broke your leg just before _____ (fill in the blank with your favorite activity). You've been looking forward to this activity for months.

d. You were sure you would get the promotion, best grade in class, scholarship, or big sale, but you were blind-sided when it was given to someone else. This really affects your future expectations.

e. The person you voted for lost the election, and now you are worried about what this will mean to your community, to your income, to your education, or to your principles.

6. **Faith Challenge.** Explain to someone what you are learning in the class: about the chain reaction that begins with praise. Use the graphic (below) to help you.

PART 2: CHAPTER 7

Aim It! Flame It!

For believers, fear presents an opportunity to choose to focus on God and stand in faith.

A battle has been going on throughout the ages of man ever since Eve and Adam chose to believe Satan's lies in the Garden of Eden. Disguised as a snake, he challenged them to look at the world as if they, not God, were the major players in the game. Satan presented a "no-confidence" vote in God by hinting that God was not good and couldn't be trusted (Genesis 3).

We've been falling for the devil's lies ever since.

Living in faith doesn't mean we won't face adversity (John 16:33). We will, but God doesn't leave us to fight battles using only our own puny strength. He's given us a weapon we can wield even in the worst hardship: the simple act of praising Him (Psalm 8:2). **And if we carry the weapon of praise with us every day, then faith is also our regular companion.**

FAITH IS LEARNED ON THE JOURNEY

Until God rescued the Hebrews from slavery in Egypt, they had few life options and lived at the fickle will of their owners, so they were novices in making choices of any kind, including faith and trust. Although these slaves had dreamt about freedom, the reality in the desert failed to match their expectation. After 40 years of wandering in the wilderness, totally dependent on God for survival, a faithless generation died out, and their children continued learning "how-to-choose" lessons in faith and obedience. As they prepared to enter the Promised Land, God told them that they would still have to depend on God for survival (Deuteronomy 11:10-12, NLT).

The Middle East, the Promised Land, has experienced unreliable weather patterns, drought, and famine throughout its history. God reminded the Israelites of this: that He had cared for the land and for them in the past, and He would provide their needs now and in the future. God gave His people a gift that they didn't earn because He loved them and desired to be in close relationship with them. He added a warning: "Remember the law of truth or consequences."

> *If you carefully obey the commands I am giving you today, and if you love the Lord your God and serve him with all your heart and soul, then he will send the rains in their proper seasons…But be careful. Don't let your heart be deceived so that you turn away from the Lord and serve and worship other gods. If you do, the Lord's anger will burn against you. He will shut up the sky and hold back the rain, and the ground will fail to produce its harvests.* (Deuteronomy 11:13-14 & 16-17, NLT)

The Promised Land was a testing ground of faith for the Israelites, both personally and nationally. As believers, we, too, live in a Promised Land designed to nurture faith—our world is in chaos, but God is in control. When we forget that, fear is our constant companion.

Recent history reveals our world's continual disarray: devastation as a result of the Vietnam War from 1955-1975; chaos when the Soviet Union dissolved in 1989; North Korea and Iran's nuclear threats in 2012; and in 2020, the COVID-19 virus made many of us afraid to leave our homes. Terrorism is a major topic of conversation, and headlines warn of natural disasters that will disrupt life as we know it, bringing us all back to the dark ages. Even a major segment of our entertainment is focused on zombies and end-of-the world scenarios.

Faith can seem unreachable in this hopeless modern-day wilderness, and the devil constantly plays the "no-confidence" card that tells us: "Grow up! Nobody's going to save you. If you want anything, you have to go after it for yourself."

"Grow up?!" The world equates maturity to that time we reach the ability to live on our own and are free from parental control or the need of assistance. Our young people can't wait for individual freedom and a driver's license. But is this God's definition of maturity?

Spiritual maturity is the opposite of self-dependence. **True faith is the recognition of our total dependence on God that frees us from trying to make things happen in our own strength.**

> *This day I call the heavens and the earth as witnesses against you that I have set before you, life and death, blessings and curses. Now choose life, so that you and your children may live.* (Deuteronomy 30:19, NLT)

To reach and live in the Promised Land, the Hebrew ex-slaves had to choose to follow God as a daily habit, to believe that what God promises, God delivers. We are on the same journey.

CHRIST'S FAITH IN US

FEAR SEPARATES US FROM FAITH. What causes us to step outside of our sanctuary in Christ? Why do we abandon our renewed minds, move away from the flames of our faith, and revert to our old identities? What makes us forget whose we are and choose to live separated from God as our old sinful selves? The devil schemes to take over our lives even though, in faith, we have been empowered in Christ to overcome our "former selves."

> *The sinful nature wants to do evil, which is just the opposite of what the Spirit wants. And the Spirit gives us desires that are the opposite of what the sinful nature desires. These two forces are constantly fighting each other, so you are not free to carry out your good intentions.* (Galatians 5:17, NLT)

This is serious stuff. We are in a battle every day. There's a reason that the most common greeting from God's messengers in scripture is "Don't be afraid." God said it to Gideon and his tiny army (Judges 7), to King Jehoshaphat and the people of Judah (2 Chronicles 20), and it's what Jesus said to the disciples on a wave-tossed boat in the middle of a stormy lake (Matthew 14). God has the same message for us, *"Don't be afraid."*

To us, fear may appear to be a prudent reaction to danger, but it is actually a serious firewall that stands between us and the flames of our faith. Remember, the devil uses fear as an offensive weapon to block us from the truth that God loves us and is in control of our lives, our communities, our nations, and the world. Fear is the devil's weapon.

We may be stuffed full of knowledge about God, but unless we are in a heart-relationship with him, a head full of information does not bring about a transformation. Theories and ideas are not the answer. If you want to hear this truth from Jesus' mouth, read his interchange with religious leaders (Matthew 21) who knew God's law, but didn't know God's heart.

Fear controls our thoughts and actions. Here are a few examples. Even though you know how to swim, you are still afraid of bodies of water. You know your neighbor's dog is friendly, but when it barks, you cower behind the fence. You can debate Biblical themes and theology, but don't recognize that it is God who picks you up and carries you when you can't go on. The devil knows that the deep canyon between knowledge and relationship is a great place for an ambush, and fear can freeze us in place.

Head knowledge might include attending a once-a-week church service, the ability to recite the names of the books of the Old and New Testaments, or enough knowledge to explain the fine points of theology. On the other hand, a relationship with God is a daily conversation, a hand-in-hand walk through the garden of your life, and a desire to be in God's presence. Head knowledge is good, but it is not enough.

But, do not be afraid.

For believers, **fear presents an opportunity to choose to focus on God and stand in faith.** Often, it is when we are out of human options, when we are desperate, afraid, and backed into a corner that we turn to God for help.

- Moses and the escaped slaves had the Red Sea in front of them and a furious Pharaoh and his army behind them. It wasn't logical, but Moses raised his staff in faith (Exodus 14).

- Naaman didn't travel to see Elisha because of his superior medical knowledge, but because he was God's prophet. This proud and mighty warrior had contracted a fatal illness, and fear prompted him to obey God through Elisha and wash seven times in the Jordan River (2 Kings 5).

- Peter's fellow believers were persecuted and terrified, and fear prompted them to gather together to pray desperately for help (Acts 12).

- Threatened by a mob, severely beaten by city officials, Paul and Silas sat in the inner dungeon with their feet in stocks. Bleeding, and in pain, with no hope that tomorrow would be any different, they defied fear and accessed their faith through singing songs of praise (Acts 16).

Fear. All of the faith-filled people in the above list experienced fear, but they didn't let it distract them from what they knew to be true: that they all were united with Christ (Galatians 2:20). We are branches that are attached to The Vine (John 15:5), and whatever it is that we are attached to forms our spirit and shapes how we live. Attached to the vine, we grow bigger and bigger in our faith; we keep expanding our capacity to hold the fullness of God inside us. Fear is such a puny weapon when we are full of God.

KEEP GOD FRONT AND CENTER IN EVERY FRAME. In this age of selfies, our faces are part of almost every picture we take—whether at home or in Rome; sitting alone or on the phone; even at a game, we're in the frame. Our faces are front and center in our podcasts as we talk from the front seat of a car or while walking through the neighborhood. We view the world with ourselves in the middle. Our backs are to The Light, and in front of us is a great big shadow, so we are afraid, and our thoughts, words and actions reflect this.

What are you looking at today? Identify your unbelief, contrast it with God's truth, and choose faith. And if faith feels out of reach, praising God will give you access to the fire that God laid inside you.

Our world-fixated eyes can be so out of focus that we don't recognize Jesus when he's right next to us. That's what Jesus' disciples discovered when a storm hit as they sailed across a lake (Matthew 14). Strong winds and heavy waves promised to swamp their boat and drown these experienced sailors. When they saw a man-like figure walking across the waves toward them, they imagined their own Rabbi was a ghost. They were so panicked that they didn't even recognize His voice.

Jesus called out, *"Don't be afraid. Take courage. I am here."* Only Peter responded boldly, but added a caveat: "IF it is really you, tell me to come to you." When Jesus told him to come, Peter jumped out of the boat full of trust in the power and presence of God. A few steps later, he let the raging water capture his attention and got a good soaking. However, when Peter once again saw his Lord in the middle of the frame—faith restored—he walked on the water holding the hand of the Savior.

Peter knew his Rabbi's voice, and recognized it was Jesus even though it was humanly impossible for him to be there. All the others were immobilized by fear, but Peter chose to believe it was Jesus and acted in faith. Yes, he lost it momentarily and got a little wet, but when he looked at Jesus again, his faith was restored.

Another example of wandering focus is found in Mark 9. Jesus (with Peter, James, and John) joined the crowd surrounding the remaining disciples who were being cross-examined by religious scholars. "What's this argument about?" Jesus asked. A man spoke from the crowd, "It's about my son. He is possessed by a demon, and your disciples were unable to cast it out." Both the disciples' and father's fear and confusion separated them from their faith in God's all-powerful healing presence.

We are like all-wet Peter, the other disciples, and the desperate father. We still see a ghost walking on waves or focus on "what if"

Chapter 7: Aim It! Flame It!

rather than on God. We are born again, we know His promises, but there are raging waves between us and our faith. And, like Peter and this father, we need God's help to choose to believe, to access our faith.

Peter cried for help, and Jesus held out his hand and pulled him out of the water. The boy's father asked for help to believe, and Jesus gave him what he needed and healed his son. Jesus didn't berate Peter or this father for their lack of faith; He helped them light the fire.

Jesus' message to us is clear: I am here, and IF you're having trouble, if you're stuck on "IF you can help," remember that I have given you a weapon that defeats fear and ignites your faith. It's called praise.

Jesus holds out his hand to us as He did to Peter. "Hear my voice; feel my touch. Don't be afraid, because when I'm in the picture, you have nothing to fear. And I'm always in the picture."

CHOOSE TO STRIKE THE MATCH. Faith doesn't guarantee comfort or prosperity—it is something we have to fight for, to choose over and over again—to wear a praise habit every day. Although joy is part of the journey, we will also experience lows, frustrations, and disappointments.

> *Dear friends, although I was very eager to write to you about the salvation we share, I felt compelled to write and urge you to contend for the faith that was once for all entrusted to God's holy people... by building yourselves up in your most holy faith and praying in the Holy Spirit, keep yourselves in God's love as you wait for the mercy of our Lord Jesus Christ to bring you to eternal life.* (Jude 3, 20-21, NIV)

Perhaps God has placed us in hostile places and situations to grow our faith, as He did for the Hebrews. We can't rely on the faith of parents or the fact that we belong to a Bible-believing church. We must make our own choices, own our own faith, and maintain our own relationship with the Lord. And God has placed in each of us the fire of faith as well as the tool that will light the blaze. We have to choose to strike the match.

We need to know God, hear his voice, and nurture our relationship with Him—attach ourselves to Him—as if it's the most important thing ever, because it is! God wants us to look at Him. Focus on Him. Delight in Him with praise and worship.

Praising God ignites the flames of our faith, focuses us on God our Father, and our relationship with Him grows stronger. These are the first two steps in a Biblical chain reaction in which each action activates the next, so that when we pray, God releases His power and authority to overcome evil, and we will reign and rule with Christ on earth and forever in heaven.

> We praise God because it is right, because it is appropriate, and because it is commanded. But praising God also has a radical effect on us.
> ~ David Jeremiah, *31 Days to Happiness: How to Find What Really Matters in Life,* W Publishing Group, Nashville, 2018, p298

Explore and Exercise

1. The Israelites were delighted to escape from slavery in Egypt, yet they still struggled with their faith in the God who had rescued them. We do too. When conflicts hit, we often choose as poorly as did our spiritual forefathers.

   a. What lessons did God want the Hebrews to learn during their 40 years of wandering in the desert? How did the geography of the Promised Land play a part in their training?

   b. Do you think that adversity was usually the root cause of the Israelites' choice to worship other gods? What would you say prompted them to repeatedly turn away from their faith?

   c. Which comes first: obedience or faith? Can you separate them? Can either faith or obedience exist alone, without the presence of the other?

2. If you looked up the word "maturity," the world's definition would be something like this: "the ability to respond to the environment in an appropriate manner; to behave according to the circumstances and the culture of the society one lives in. Maturity comes with experience and age."

   a. Compare this to the definition of mature faith (total dependence on God). Are there any similarities? What are the differences?

   b. What do we have to give up to have a true mature faith, and how could we do that?

3. John Calvin said God is the pilot of our lives. "Seeing that a pilot steers the ship in which we sail, who will never allow us to perish even in the midst of shipwrecks, there is no reason why our minds should be overwhelmed with fear and overcome with weariness."

a. Why do you think that the phrase, "Don't be afraid," is the most common command in the Bible?

b. What happens inside of us when we give in to fear?

c. Do you think fear and faith can exist inside you at the same time? Explain.

d. How do you combat fear? Can you share an example?

4. **What enemies, foes, and evil avengers are you facing in your spiritual battles right now?** Take a few minutes to think about your unique struggles. Fill in the examples below to help you gain a clear picture of your personal battles.

   a. My Enemies are: _____
   (Examples: pride, lust, anger, despair, poor self-worth, fear, selfishness…)

   b. My Firewalls are: _____
   (Examples: I have a hard time trusting that God will fulfill his promises to me. I'm not sure that God could really love me. There's no time in my busy life to spend with God. I'm really drawn to something other than God.)

   c. My Foes are: _____
   (Examples: a demon of despair, doubt, depression, procrastination, confusion, complacence…)

   Now that you have identified your unique enemies, firewalls, and foes, use the faith challenge below to prepare for battle. God's already given us the victory!

5. **Faith Challenge.** Be proactive and prepare, because you will be called to the battleground over and over. Hard times will come, so develop some match-striking habits to use when praise is the last thing you feel like doing. Remember to use praise as a weapon, as the catalyst that starts the chain reaction which aims and flames your faith.

   a. Instead of recounting a list of what made today so miserable, look for, make a list, and speak about the blessings and promises that brought you through it.

b. In Acts 27, we read the story of a centurion and his troops who were escorting Paul by ship to Rome for his trial. When a delay left them stranded in a poor harbor due to possible dangerous winter travel, Paul warned him, "I see only disaster ahead for cargo and ship—to say nothing of our lives—if we put out to sea now." However, the centurion chose to ignore the warning, and they put to sea. As Paul predicted, the ship was caught up in a furious storm. They readied a lifeboat, dumped the cargo, and finally in desperation threw all their provisions and tackle overboard. For over two week, the waves and wind battered their ship, and in the storm's deep darkness, all those on board lost all hope of rescue.

Paul gathered them together all 276 people and said, "Don't be afraid; nobody's going to die. An Angel of the Lord visited me last night and told me that I was going to have my day in Caesar's court and that everyone sailing with me was going to make it."

A few days later, the sailors feared they were going to run aground. They attempted to lower a lifeboat to sneak away from ship, but Paul told the centurion and his soldiers, "If these sailors don't stay with the ship, we're all going down." The soldiers cut the lines to the lifeboat so it drifted away.

Then Paul encouraged everyone to eat some breakfast. "This is the fourteenth day we've gone without food. But I urge you to eat something now. You will need strength for the rescue ahead. You're going to come out of this without even a scratch!" He broke the bread, gave thanks to God, and they all ate heartily.

But things seemed to go from bad to worse. The crew saw an island with a beach, set a sail, and tried to run aground, but it didn't work. The ship got stuck on a reef and began to break apart...but everyone made it to the beach safely.

i. Do you think Paul could have been afraid before the Angel of the Lord visited him? Why do you think the centurion and his soldiers believed Paul when he reported the Angel's words?

ii. Even when all on board made it safely to shore after the shipwreck, the Lord wasn't finished revealing his power. Read Acts 28:1-10 to hear the story of further miracles. When you find yourself afraid, without hope, and unsure that God holds you in his hands, reread Acts 27 and 28. Picture yourself on that boat, and watch God in all His power save your life. Strike the match. Aim and flame.

c. Read the stories of other Heroes of faith—Joshua, Ruth, and Moses—paying special attention to how they made it through desperate times in their lives. Pattern your faith on theirs.

d. Personalize Bible verses and read them aloud. Use the samples below or choose your own verses.

   i. *The Lord is not slow in keeping His promise, as some understand slowness. Instead He is patient with [your name], not wanting [me] to perish, but to come to repentance.* (2 Peter 3:9, NIV)

   ii. *And [I] heard a loud voice from the throne saying, "Look! God's dwelling place is now among the people, and he dwells in [your name]. I will be one of his people, and God himself will be with [me] and be [my] God.* (Revelation 21:3, NIV)

   iii. *[I will not] be afraid or discouraged, for the Lord will personally go ahead of [me]. He will be with [me]; he will neither fail [me] nor abandon [me].* (Deuteronomy 31:8, NLT)

   iv. *And [I] know that God causes everything to work together for [my] good because [I] love God and am called according to his purpose for [me].* (Romans 8:28, NLT)

   v. *But now, [I or your name)] will listen to the Lord who created me, the one who formed [me] who says, "Do not be afraid, for*

I have ransomed you. I have called you [your name]; *you are mine. When* [I] *go through deep waters,* [God] *will be with* (me). *When* [I] *go through rivers of difficulty,* [I] *will not drown. When* [I] *walk through the fire of oppression,* [I] *will not be burned up; the flames will not consume* [me]…*For the Lord,* [my] *God, the Holy One of Israel,* [is my] *Savior.* (Isaiah 43:1-3a, NLT)

vi. *This is what the Lord says* [to me]: *"Do not be afraid! Don't be discouraged by this mighty army, for the battle is not yours, but God's. Tomorrow, march out against* [whatever enemies you are fighting]. *You will find them…But you will not even need to fight. Take your positions; then stand still and watch the Lord's victory. I, the Lord, am with* [you or your name]." (2 Chronicles 20:15-17, NLT)

PART 3
Pray Powerful Prayers

Prayer undergirds action with God's strength.

Praise, faith, and prayer are interrelated and inseparable. Prayer flows out of faith and trust in God alone. Praise ignites the faith-fire that God has already placed in us. So, these three—praise, faith, and prayer—are the building blocks of a relationship between God the Father and His children and heirs. The power comes from God and is released in answer to our prayers.

We don't have to know how to pray a perfect prayer or wait until we think we are "good enough." Our prayers may be unfocused or muddied by our fleshly desires. We might start to pray with an attempt to manipulate God, and end up opening up our hearts to His will, which is greater, wiser, and more intelligent than our own (Psalm 62:5). We don't have to be a theologian, a pastor, or a televangelist to pray powerful prayers—we have the Holy Spirit to guide us when we don't know how or what to pray for.

In the same way, the Spirit helps us in our weakness. We do not know what we ought to pray for, but the Spirit himself intercedes for us with groans that words cannot express. And he who searches our hearts knows the mind of the Spirit, because the Spirit intercedes for the saints in accordance with God's will. (Romans 8:26-27, NIV)

God wants us to wear our daily praise and faith habit boldly—with confidence and trust—so that we can pray powerful prayers that He wants to answer because we have delighted in Him!

> True prayer is neither a mere mental exercise nor a vocal performance. It is far deeper than that—it is spiritual transaction with the Creator of Heaven and Earth. ~ Charles Spurgeon

PART 3: CHAPTER 8

Story Time, Past and Present

As they were praying,
they heard the voice of God.

PETER AND PRAYERS FOR POWER

A New Testament Story of Prayer: Acts 10

Peter was a fisherman until Jesus chose him to be his disciple, and challenged Peter's understanding of faith: follow the rules and regulations. Instead, his Rabbi demanded a radical attitude change. Jesus taught, "God's love is a gift to all." Sinners, lepers, tax-collectors, Romans, and prostitutes received Divine grace and mercy alongside high-born and righteous Jews. It took three years of intensive transformation while following in Jesus' footsteps to change Peter into a fisher of men.

After Jesus' death and resurrection, Peter traveled throughout the land to support Jewish believers of The Way. While in Joppa, he stayed at the home of a tanner, a choice that repudiated his former lifestyle of adhering to rules and regulations.

> HISTORICAL NOTE: Ancient Jewish zoning laws required tanneries to be located at the edge of town—downwind—because the stench was awful. Animal hides were treated with foul mixtures of animal or human waste and harsh chemicals, and often the flesh remaining on a hide was left to rot. The disgusting odor permeated the clothes, skin, and house of a tanner. As a result, tanners were treated as outcasts from polite society and were pushed to the fringes of Jewish religious life.

Clearly, Peter didn't choose to stay at the tanner's house for personal comfort or societal gain, but his carefully-selected residence reflected the New Covenant in Jesus Christ.

Following the Rabbi's example, Peter found a quiet place to be **by himself and pray**—the rooftop's advantage could have been the clean breeze coming off the Mediterranean. After some time in prayer, Peter grew hungry and asked for lunch. As he waited, the presence of the Lord knocked him to his knees. In a trance, Peter saw a vessel full of animals being lowered down from heaven, and God's voice told him, "Get up, Peter. Kill and eat."

"Surely not!" Peter exclaimed. Frankly, he was shocked at God's command—hadn't he always abided by Hebrew laws of purity? "I have never eaten anything impure or unclean."

The voice answered, "Do not call anything impure that God has made clean." Immediately, the vessel disappeared.

As Peter tried to return to the reality of the rooftop, the vision happened again. Two more times he saw the vessel full of all sorts of animals and heard the voice. His dismayed response and God's rebuke were repeated just as before.

"Three times," Peter groaned from his knees. "Three times means this is important," Peter muttered. "But I don't understand, Lord," he asked. "Is this about Jewish dietary laws?"

Deep in thought, Peter paid no attention to the knocking and raised voices at the house gate, until the Holy Spirit spoke again. "Simon, three men have arrived, so get up and go downstairs. Do not hesitate to go with them, for I have sent them."

On stiff legs, Peter descended the outside stairway to the interior courtyard and approached the three men knocking at the gate.

"I'm the one you're looking for," Peter told them. "Why have you come?"

A Roman soldier replied, "We have come from Cornelius the centurion. He is a righteous and God-fearing man, who is respected by all the Jewish people. **As he was praying**, a holy angel appeared and told him to summon you to his house so that he could hear what you have to say."

Peter glanced up toward heaven; "Ah. I see." Opening the gate, he beckoned the visitors to enter. "Please come in and rest yourselves as I prepare for the journey."

Peter and some elders from Joppa set out early the next morning for the two-day walk to Caesarea. They found a large group of people waiting for them at Cornelius' house. In his usual direct manner, Peter told the crowd. *"You are well aware that it is against our law for a Jew to associate with or visit a Gentile. But God has shown me that I should not call anyone impure or unclean. So when I was sent for, I came without raising any objection. May I ask why you sent for me?"* (Acts 10:28-29, TPT)

> *Cornelius answered, "Three days ago I was in my house praying at this hour, at three in the afternoon. Suddenly a man in shining clothes stood before me and said, 'Cornelius, God has heard your prayer and remembered your gifts to the poor. Send to Joppa for Simon who is called Peter.' So I sent for you immediately, and it was good of you to come. Now we are all here in the presence of God to listen to everything the Lord has commanded you to tell us."* (Acts 10:30-33, MSG)

Then Peter began to speak to Cornelius and everyone there.

> *"I now realize how true it is that God does not show favoritism only to the Jews, but accepts people from every nation who fear him and do what is right. It is clear to me that you know the message God sent to the people of Israel, announcing the good news of peace through Jesus Christ, who is Lord of all. You know what has happened throughout the province of Judea, beginning in Galilee after the baptism that John the Baptist preached—how God anointed Jesus of Nazareth with the Holy Spirit and power, and how he went around doing good and healing all who were under the power of the devil, because God was with him.*
>
> *"We are witnesses of everything Jesus did in the country of the Jews and in Jerusalem. They killed Him by hanging Him on a cross, but God raised Him from the dead on the third day and chose us to be witnesses—those of us who ate and drank with Him after he rose from the dead. He commanded us to preach to the people and to testify that He is the one whom God appointed as judge of the living and*

the dead. And it's not just us saying this. The prophets have long testified that everyone who believes in Him receives forgiveness of sins through His name." (Acts 10:34-43, NIV)

While Peter was still speaking these words, **the Holy Spirit came on all who heard** the message. This astonished the Jewish men who had come with Peter, but they couldn't deny what they, themselves, were witnessing, Gentile believers were speaking in tongues and praising God.

Then Peter said, "Surely no one can object if we baptize these believers with water. They have received the Holy Spirit just as we have."

All the worshippers in Cornelius' house were baptized in the name of Jesus Christ. Many gathered around Peter after their baptism and pleaded, "Please stay with us for a few days and teach us more about our Savior." So Peter and the believers from Joppa stayed with them for a few days.

For the eyes of the Lord are on the righteous, and his ears are attentive to their prayer." (1 Peter 3:12a, NIV)

Cornelius had a **regular prayer time** each day.
Peter habitually **went apart from others to pray**.
These two men took time to **be in God's presence**,
and it was **as they were praying that they heard His voice.**

PRAYERS FOR PETER

A New Testament Story of Prayer: Acts 12

Hoping to murder the prophesied Messiah, Herod the Great had murdered all the boys two years old and younger in Bethlehem. His grandson, Herod Agrippa, showed the same hunger for control and power.

Herod Agrippa came from Rome to rule over the Palestine territory ten years after Jesus' death and resurrection. In order to cement his power base in the area, Herod piously acted as an observer of Jewish practices. He also ruthlessly oppressed all disruptive minorities. He even ordered that James, the son of Zebedee and brother of John, be beheaded by sword, an execution method normally used to punish murderers. This action caused Herod's approval rating to skyrocket among the Jewish elite, and so this politically shrewd ruler determined to keep up the pressure. Herod had Peter arrested during the Festival of Unleavened Bread, a time when Jews from across the country were celebrating in Jerusalem.

To publicly show how pious he was, Herod appointed four squads (of four soldiers each) to insure that this important prisoner could not escape before the public trial that was scheduled to take place after the seven-day Jewish festival. Two soldiers were chained to Peter in his cell, while two others guarded the entrance. To maintain maximum alertness, the guards changed shifts every three hours during the night.

For seven days, **the church gathered to pray earnestly** for their imprisoned leader—the only weapon they had against the power of the Roman army. And for seven days Peter endured constant agony, a stench strong enough to be tasted, heavy chains, manacles that cut into his wrists and ankles, and nearly inedible food. His attempts to speak with the guards were painfully silenced, for their own lives depended on delivering Peter to trial. The nights were the worst as fear's claws raked him, so that **he prayed continually for strength and peace.**

The night before the public trial, Peter slept slumped against his chains until something-that-was-not-fear roused him. Peter only groaned when he felt a kick in the ribs, until a second, more-insistent kick followed. He squeezed his eyes shut to block out the bright light that filled the cell until the light-source spoke, and the manacles fell from his arms and legs with a loud clank.

"Be quick, get up!" an angel urged Peter as he struggled to his feet. "Put on your clothes and sandals." Peter did so, freezing in fear when he tripped over the guard out cold on the floor. The angel urged him on, "Don't worry. Wrap your cloak around you, and follow me."

Peter still wasn't sure whether or not he was dreaming as he crept silently behind the angel. The guards at the entrance to the cell block looked straight at them without recognition.

"Can this be real?" Peter thought to himself as the iron gate leading to the city slowly opened, and they left the prison grounds. The angel disappeared after they had walked the length of one street.

"It is real! I'm free," he whispered in awe. "Now I know without a doubt that the Lord answered our prayers and sent his angel to rescue me from Herod's clutches."

Peter furtively made his way to the house of Mary the mother of John (Mark) where **many people had gathered and were praying.** A servant named Rhoda answered his knock, but when she recognized Peter's voice, she was so overjoyed she ran back without opening the door exclaiming, "Peter is at the door!"

"You're out of your mind," they told her. When she kept insisting that it was so, they said, "It must be his angel."

Hiding in the shadowed doorway, Peter quietly knocked again. "Rhoda! Rhoda, come back and let me in!"

Finally, the door opened a crack, and shadowed faces peered out at him. Hands pulled him inside and re-latched the door. A small candle was uncovered and held near his face, and Peter heard Rhoda's voice. "See! He is real."

His friends were astonished and gathered around him asking questions in loud whispers. Peter signaled for quiet, and once they had moved away from the door, described how the Lord had brought him out of prison.

"This will be the first place the soldiers will look for me," Peter told them. "Tell James and the other brothers and sisters about this," and then he left through the back gate to hide elsewhere.

In the morning, the desperate soldiers had no idea what had become of Peter. After Herod had a thorough search made for him and did not find him, he cross-examined the guards and ordered that they be executed.

[Jesus asked his disciples,] *"And will not God bring about justice for his chosen ones, who cry out to him day and night? Will he keep putting them off? I tell you, he will see that they get justice, and quickly."* (Luke 18:6-8, NIV)

For seven days, the believers persistently gathered together to pray.
Peter prayed from his prison cell.
God responded with an angel rescue.

WE SHOULD HAVE LEFT AN HOUR AGO

A Modern-Day True Story of Prayer

I stay with Mom and Dad
For a week
Before his brain surgery.
We cry a little,
Talk a lot,
Pray all the time:
The three of us together,
With everyone who stops by,
Or calls on the phone.

Packing up
Two distraught people
To go to San Francisco
For surgery
Is only accomplished in spurts
Between
Answering the doorbell
And the telephone
Which rings again.
"This is the last time I'll answer it!"

Dad talks to a colleague.
I load the trunk,

Check off items on the list with Mom,
Walk through the house—
Closing latches, locks, windows—
Then rearrange the trunk.
I stand in front of Dad,
I pace.
Mom gets on the other line,
Then calls to me,
"Get on the phone.
We'll pray for a safe trip."

I kick the sofa,
Grind my teeth,
Take a deep breath,
Pick up the phone
To listen
While others pray
For the rain to ease,
For energy,
For safe travel
While I watch the minute hand on my watch.

I grip the steering wheel as we set out
To traverse unfamiliar territory
Masked by fog and rain
And find a tunnel of sunshine
on clearly marked roads
that lead straight to our destination.

Thank you, God,
For answering a prayer grudgingly offered.

~ Kathleen Evenhouse, 1993

Explore and Exercise

1. Both Peter and the Centurion Cornelius scheduled daily prayer time (Acts 10).

    a. Why do you think both Peter and Cornelius were convinced that it was the Lord's voice that they heard?

    b. What did the way Cornelius responded to the angel's message tell us about him?

    c. Share a time when you heard God's voice in some way speaking to you. Did you recognize it at the time or only realize it was His voice when you looked back at the situation?

2. Peter had been privileged to be the first to preach the full gospel on Pentecost Sunday (Acts 2). Since that time, the apostles and their disciples had been preaching to Jews and Gentile converts to Judaism, and Peter traveled through the country teaching and encouraging these recent converts to The Way (Acts 6:2-3).

    a. To the Jewish people of Bible times, the number 3 represented divine wholeness, completeness, and perfection. Read Matthew 26:36 & 75; John 21:1-19. What special significance did the number 3 have for Peter in his relationship with Jesus?

    b. How did God reinforce his vision to Peter?

    c. What do Peter's first words to Cornelius and his friends tell you about the internal battle that was going on his head (Acts 10:28-29 & 34-36)? Explain your thoughts as to why, despite the long Jewish tradition of separation, did Peter agree to enter the house of a Roman?

    d. Have you ever been confused by God's message until He reaffirmed His will for you in a way similar to what Peter experienced? Share this experience.

3. Group prayer knits believers together and encourages the burdened (Galatians 6:2; James 5:13-18). It is also a way in which we worship God together, as His called-out people, to give Him praise, to seek His will, to confess our sins, and to confess our reliance on Him. When believers pray together, the result is unity, humility, thanksgiving, confession of sin, intercession, and discovery of God's will.

   a. Do you think the Lord's Prayer (Matthew 6:9-13) is intended to be prayed by a group or individually. Give examples from the prayer that support your choice.

   b. When we join our voices together as Peter's fellow believers did when Peter was imprisoned (Acts 12), are we more likely to receive the outcome we prayed for? What are the benefits of praying with others?

4. Have any of you have realized mid-prayer that you were attempting to tell God what you wanted Him to do. How did you hear God's answer" Did He say, "Yes," "No," or "Wait?" Perhaps God had a whole different plan in mind for you. Share that experience.

5. In the poem, a daughter was caught up in schedules, worry, and getting on the road. Her parents were thinking only of people, God, and prayer. They prayed together, but the daughter was focused on her frustration even while praying, yet God blessed them with good weather and smooth travel right up to the door of the hospital (in the days before GPS and smart phones).

   a. Why do we sometimes avoid prayer?

   b. Why do we sometimes view prayer as our last resort, after we've tried everything else we can do?

   c. It was only out of obedience that the daughter joined the prayer. She let her circumstances distract her from God, but God's response was powerful and clear.

      i. What does that tell us about God and how He desires to be in relationship with us?

> ii. Do you believe that the Holy Spirit would speak for you in a prayer offered in obedience, without you having a current emotional commitment?

6. **Prayer Challenge**: Read Joel 2:28. Prayer is a time when God reveals things to us, engages us in conversation, and changes us from the inside out. If you long to experience Joel's prophecy in your own life, try incorporating some of these ideas about prayer.

    a. Begin with praise, developing it as a habit by praying seven times a day to light the fire of your faith. When faith is blazing, you can really believe that the power of the Holy Spirit changes everything. In this trust, prayer becomes exciting, something you anticipate rather than a task you dutifully endure when you need to ask for something.

    b. Ask the Holy Spirit to take over your life completely and willingly make room by kicking down the walls of your worldly self. Readily accept the gifts God has for you in whatever way He chooses to give them.

    c. Be persistent. Don't just ask once, but spend regular sessions with God asking to discern the Holy Spirit's voice in your life. Listen to and obey His promptings.

    d. Identify something in your life that distracts you from making space to experience intimacy with the Holy Spirit. It could be hobbies, habits, your smart phone, or computer. Spend some time away from the distractions in your life to help you hear the Holy Spirit's voice.

PART 3: CHAPTER 9

What Is Prayer?

"If only we knew what was happening when we pray, we would never cease to pray." ~Louie Giglio

What is your picture of "prayer?"

- A vending machine: you insert your quarters and God gives you what you ask for.
- A structured liturgy that you repeat over and over.
- A special position: on your knees, hands folded, and eyes closed.
- Something you do with your children at bedtime.

Do you have a special voice and vocabulary that you use only when you pray out loud? Are your prayers all memorized or recited from a prayer book? Does prayer always have to involve words?

Prayer, like praise, can become a habit that we wear, but if we are stuck on a particular format, every habit hanging in our prayer closet will have a same color or style. In this chapter, we'll explore what prayer is. Then we can expand our prayer closets in order to hold a variety of habits that enable us to pray in every situation.

PRAYER IS A CONVERSATION WITH GOD

Take a minute to consider how you would explain prayer to someone who has no prior experience or knowledge of it. You might use one of the phrases below, but as you do, you will also realize that you have only scratched the surface.

- Prayer may seem complicated, but it is simply talking with God.
- Prayer is not passive reflection within ourselves, but it is a direct address to God.
- Prayer is the communication of the human soul with the Lord who created the soul.
- Prayer is a two-way street between us and God—we both ask and receive, speak and listen.

Do you ever wonder about the God to whom you are praying? Is He real? Is He powerful? Does He care about you? If we wrote down everything mankind has ever learned about God, it would still only tell us a sliver of who He is. God reveals Himself in the Bible, and we can also see Him in the universe He created. Look up at the sky. Our sun, a minor star, emits the same amount of power as 450 eight-cylinder automobile engines per square yard—what power! God made all the stars in the universe, and He directs their movement, guides the constellations through the seasons, and regulates His creation with laws He designed to form and maintain the universe (Job 38). We, on the other hand, are so small and limited in perspective that if we hold up a circle as small as a dime at arm's length, we block out fifteen million stars from our view. Go outside and try it yourself. Who is this God we pray to? He is the Creator that brought our whole universe into being (Genesis 1), and He is big enough to handle anything we bring to Him.

Yet this immense, powerful, infinite God not only knows each one of us, He loves us (John 3:16). He wants to have a relationship with each of us, not because we earned it or deserve it, but because of His love and mercy. His love doesn't depend on the depths of our faith or the holiness of our thoughts—God loves us just as we are (Romans 5:8). God's love demolished the sin barrier when Jesus Christ came to earth to pay the price for our sins.

God also shows Himself to us as One God with three distinct personages we call the Trinity: Father, Son, and Holy Spirit. This Trinitarian family unit is a never-ending Circle of Love, and our Father invites all those who believe in Him to join this Circle of Love as His children and heirs.

> *See how very much our Father loves us, for he calls us his children, and that is what we are!* (1 John 3:1, NLT)

God is faithful (1 Corinthians 1:9). Our relationship with Him is not a contract that says if we break our part of the agreement (and we will), that God is free to break His part of the deal. God loves us, and He established the conditions and guarantees the results.

We don't earn God's love or salvation, but that doesn't mean we don't have to put forth any effort into our relationship with Him. We don't pray in order to understand ourselves, to figure out what makes us tick so that we can strive to do better. **We choose to pray to God, to spend time in His presence, because He is the very center of our being—not our feelings, the meaning of life, or even our souls.** We choose, and He gives us everything He has promised.

To whom do we pray? The Almighty, Creator, Ruler, King of Kings, Lord of Lords, Alpha and Omega, the Lamb, the Good Shepherd, the Rock, the Redeemer...God in three persons, Blessed Trinity.

Who are believers? God's beloved children and heirs.

PRAYER IS MULTIDIMENSIONAL

Prayer can be audible or silent, public or private, formal or informal. You might picture people praying with folded hands or bowed heads, kneeling, or prostrate on the floor. People may recite prayers together using written liturgy or offer them spontaneously. Prayers might be said alone or as part of a group, spoken poetically or stammered in broken sentences, articulated in a special language or in wordless cries, shouted loudly or simply whispered in rhythm with our breathing.

Considering all of these options, our simple introduction to prayer may seem inadequate. But no matter what our prayers look like, the Bible makes it clear that **the act of praying is important**. The Gospel Coalition cites 650 examples of prayers and approximately 450 answers to prayer, with scripture references. Jesus constantly communicated with His Father, and twenty-five of his prayers are noted during His years on earth. Paul mentions prayer forty-one times in the thirteen books of the New Testament that he authored.

What does prayer look like? The Bible lists five specific postures for prayer: sitting (2 Samuel 7:18), standing (Mark 11:25), kneeling, (Daniel 6:13), with one's face to the ground (Matthew 26:39), and with hands lifted up (1 Timothy 2:8). However, prayer is more than the posture we choose because we are also told to "pray continually" (1 Thessalonians 5:17), and to do that requires multiple expressions of prayer.

Praise is a form of prayer that reminds us of the great God we worship and who we are to Him. "Praying in tongues" is a gift that God gives to many of His children, in which the Holy Spirit takes over their speech (1 Corinthians 14:4). Even though the speaker or listener may find the words unintelligible, this unique language reflects close communion with the Holy Spirit who is bringing our needs to the Father.

Let's look a little deeper into some kinds of prayer that we could add to our collection.

MEDITATE. Some might associate the word "meditation" with Eastern religious practices, but it simply means "deep thinking or contemplation." As we think deeply about God's words our

Chapter 9: What Is Prayer?

understanding grows, and the Holy Spirits helps us incorporate God's words into the way we live our lives.

One model of meditation is *Lectio Divina*, a traditional monastic practice which combines scripture reading, deep contemplation, and prayer. In this style of prayer, we simply enter into a quiet space in order to focus our attention on God. This may involve a particular place: in our home, in nature, or in a specified area in a church. Or it could be more active, such as listening to or reciting Scripture as we drive or walk. Each of us can choose a thoughtful meditative practice that fits us and our lifestyle, for example: rewriting Scripture in our own words, drawing a picture or graph to express what we hear from God, researching the historical context in which the Bible was written, or figuring out how to explain to another what God's words mean to you.

> *I meditate on your precepts and consider your ways… I reach out for your commands, which I love, that I may meditate on your decrees.* (Psalm 119:15, 48, NIV)

CONFESS. When we pray in a group, we might say, "Lord, forgive our sins." However, this broad statement doesn't require individual recognition or admission of our particular failures. It is important that we identify and confess specifics in our private conversations with God. Confession helps break down inner barriers so that, with Holy Spirit help, we can grow to be more Christ-like (James 5:16). For example:

- "Forgive me, Lord, for losing my temper with the kids today. I was so focused on what I wanted, that I neglected to practice the firm-but-loving discipline that follows the patterns of Your Love for me. Help me to stop, listen to your voice, and choose a better way next time."

- "Forgive me, Lord, for gossiping about another person so judgmentally. Help me, instead, to express in my heart, words, and actions the kind of love You have for us."

- "Forgive me, Lord, for slacking off at work today, for not giving my employer my best efforts. Remind me that everything I do is for Your glory."

When we confess our sins, we also acknowledge that we need God's help to change our patterns of thoughts and behavior. We need His help and strength—our own efforts are never enough.

INTERCEDE FOR OTHERS. When Jesus was asked to cite the greatest commandment, He replied, "[1] *Love the Lord your God with all your soul and with all your mind..."* [2] *"Love your neighbor as yourself"* (Matthew 22:37). Prayer is an action of love for our neighbors.

> *I urge you, first of all, to pray for all people. Ask God to help them; intercede on their behalf, and give thanks for them.* (1 Timothy 2:1, NLT)

There are as many ways to intercede for others as there are individuals, groups, and situations. God set up a partnership system, a way for humankind to work alongside Him: we pray, and He releases His power. This is modeled in the prayer Jesus taught us to pray, *Your kingdom come. Your will be done, on earth as it is in heaven* (Matthew 6:10).

PRAY IN TONGUES. Paul gives a lengthy discourse on the gifts of the Holy Spirit in 1 Corinthians 12. He explains that the church as the Body of Christ has many different members, each of whom have been given gifts that are to be used to serve the rest of the body. One of these gifts is praying in tongues, in which a language that is unknown to the speaker is given by the Holy Spirit, and the believer talks with God in words that others cannot understand.

The Holy Spirit has given the glorious gift of tongues for th edification of the believer and the church. Another gift works in conjunction with the gift of tongues—interpretation of what is spoken. The apostle Paul presents a framework for using the gift of speaking in tongues (1 Corinthians 14: 4-5).

PRAY FOR HEALING. In response to faith-filled prayers, God acts in us spiritually, emotionally, and physically. The power of God was shown in Jesus' ministry as He healed the sick. For the disciples and for us today, God works directly through prayer. He releases this same power to us through the Holy Spirit as we pray for healing in His name (Acts 3:6-7, 16).

SILENT SOAKING PRAYER—IMMERSED IN GOD'S PRESENCE. When we engage in silent soaking prayer, we stand in a shower of God's presence and are drenched with His love and peace. Participants pray individually in a room, often with soft music and lowered lights. Designated prayer-persons go about the room from person to person, inviting the Holy Spirit to work in each one.

PRAYER AND FASTING. Before you ask, "fasting" is not the hope that time will pass quickly until we can eat again. Nor are we referring to intermittent fasting: specified periods without food as an effective weight-loss tool. Spiritual fasting has a totally different purpose.

The Bible teaches us to "fast," which means voluntarily refraining from food in order to focus on prayer and fellowship with God. When we set food aside—food is necessary for life—we are saying to God, "You are the Bread of Life, and we depend totally on you for strength, provision, and wisdom."

"Fast and pray" were King Jehoshaphat's instructions to his citizens when they faced annihilation at the hands of a vast army (2 Chronicles 20). Church members in Antioch fasted and prayed as a part of worship, and God responded by directing them to support and enable Paul and Barnabas on a mission trip (Acts 13:1-3). When the disciples could not heal a demon-possessed boy, Jesus explained, *"This kind can come out by nothing but prayer and fasting"* (Mark 9:29, NKJV).

OVERCOMING EVIL. Prayer is an essential weapon in our battle to drive out evil (Ephesians 6:18). Overcoming Evil is the next step in our chain reaction and will be discussed thoroughly in Part 4 of this book.

WHEREVER, WHENEVER—PRAY!

As persons of faith, we are called to be people of prayer, people who seek God's presence, and reflect His glory. Many believers set aside a particular time to pray, as Jesus did. However, conversation with God goes beyond a notation on our calendars for a specific time and place. Prayer plays a part in every minute and hour, every thought and word, and every action of every day and night. **Prayer is meant to permeate our lives.**

Pray continually. (1 Thessalonians 5:17, NIV)

This may seem to be an impossible task. If we closed our eyes and bowed our heads all day long, accidents would happen. To pray continually, we have to realize that there is no "one-right-way" to pray; forgetting this can lead to embarrassing situations.

I, Kathleen, was focused on including prayer throughout my day, so I decided to pray while I was working out. I warmed up, set the treadmill speed to achieve the appropriate exercise, and closed my eyes to clear my mind for prayer. Big mistake. I picked myself up from the floor behind the treadmill and, with a red face, assured everyone that I was okay. When later I admitted I had closed my eyes to pray while I walked, the trainer laughed and said, "God won't mind if you keep your eyes open."

More than a particular position or stance, prayer is an action that puts God in the center of our world, acknowledges His eternal presence, and reminds us that He is always listening. An old Jewish adage says, "You should learn from a rabbi by covering yourself in his dust." Jesus' disciples walked through the countryside with him, and in doing so, they learned to "pray continually." Jesus invites each one of us to follow in His footsteps, to be in continual communication with Him. Our goal is to become as dust-covered as possible (Ephesians 6:18).

> If only we knew what was happening when we pray, we would never cease to pray.
> ~ Louie Giglio, Twitter post from April 4, 2012

For orthodox Jews, the Western Wall in Jerusalem is a place of prayer. In fact, they believe this 50-foot stone wall is the holiest place in the world because it is the closest they can get to the Old Testament temple and the Holy of Holies. Millions of Hindus who follow Vastu are guided to place their primary deity (statue) facing south, while they face east to pray or north to do puja.

Muslims pray five times a day and face the city of Mecca as they do so.

Although Christians may designate a place and time to pray as a personal spiritual discipline, "where" Jesus-followers pray is not an issue. Why not? Because since Jesus sent the Holy Spirit to believers on Pentecost, the Holy Spirit now dwells within each and every believer—each believer is a temple that houses the Holy Spirit. Therefore, God's temple is present wherever a believer goes.

> *Do you not know that your bodies are temples of the Holy Spirit, who is in you, whom you have received from God? You are not your own; you were bought at a price. Therefore, honor God with your bodies.* (1 Corinthians 6:19-20, NIV)

During his ministry years, Jesus was surrounded constantly by people with needs. He often got up early—his only alone time—and went out into the hills to talk to His Father (Mark 1:35). Many Christians follow His example and set a time and place to be alone with God: a specific room or chair in their homes or a special space in their churches—a designated "prayer closet." This habit, an acquired mode of behavior, helps to bring us quickly into conversation with God.

The prayers of faithful believers, united together, are mighty weapons that release God's power to oppose evil in this world (Matthew 19:19-20), and the Bible is full of examples. United in prayer, believers claim Christ's victory over Satan and bring the Kingdom of God to earth "as it is in heaven." We pray with family and friends at mealtimes, with children at bedtime, and in groups of believers for special causes. We pray in church services, Bible studies, get-togethers, and potlucks.

With faith as the foundation, our prayers don't have to be eloquent, all-inclusive, or well-structured. It is not special wording or the length of our prayers that matter, but when we go to God with trusting, open hearts, He gives us the authority and power to claim His victory and affect the balance of power in all the affairs of the world.

GOD LISTENS—YOUR VOICE MATTERS

A friend asked, "When you pray, who do you address your prayer to: Father, Jesus, or Holy Spirit?" We all had different answers and reasons, but concluded that it really didn't matter, because when we pray, all members of the Trinity (the Circle of Love) hear us and are involved in the answer.

- When we pray to God the Father, we pray in Jesus' name because it is through Jesus that we have access to the throne. The Holy Spirit prompts us and assists us in our prayers.

- When we pray to Jesus, He intercedes for us with the Father (Mark 14:62). Again, the Holy Spirit is encouraging and supporting us as we pray.

- Sometimes we might only be able to repeat God's name while we cry or merely breathe in and out with His Name in our minds. When we don't have the words, are in too much pain, are in danger, or totally at the end of any human efforts, the Holy Spirit brings our wordless moans to heaven with a translation (Romans 8:26-27, NLT).

- And sometimes, as we pray, the Holy Spirit gives us a special language that is understood by Jesus and the Father.

We are in the Circle of Love by invitation, salvation, and adoption. Our prayers are heard. God releases his power and authority as we pray.

Sometimes, in spite of our prayers, it seems that the devil lands solid punch after punch. We pray and we wait. Thump. Pray and wait. Ouch! It appears to be a repetitive pattern. Is God not answering? Doesn't God love you? Could "no" really be His answer?

> *Trust in the Lord with all your heart; do not depend on your own understanding.* (Proverbs 3:5, NLT)

Have you ever gone on a road trip with kids who constantly want to stop? They take turns asking for ice cream, to play in a playground, to stretch their legs, to do anything just so long as they can get out of the car. As the adult in charge, you often say, "wait," "not yet," or "no." Why? Not because you don't hear them, you are mean, or you don't care about them. **The truth is, you have a final destination in mind, and it is very important that you help them arrive there. It would be chaos if you said "yes" to their every desire.**

> *For God has not destined us for wrath, but to obtain salvation through our Lord Jesus Christ.* (1 Thessalonians 5:9, ESV)

We have to trust that God knows more than we do; He knows what's ahead. **God has a destiny, a destination, for your life—salvation** (John 1:29). Like a loving caregiver, He will stop to encourage you (Psalm 10:17) or to quiet you on His lap until you find peace (John 14:27, 1 John 2:2). He may also stop at your request, but frowns at anything that deters you from the right path. When God says, "wait," "not yet," or "no," how will you respond?

If God has to choose between your satisfaction on earth and your heavenly salvation, what do you think His choice will be? Every time.

Praise, faith, and prayer—links in a chain reaction that sustain a deep relationship with God—bring the realization that we know God engages in our problems. In prayer, we remember who God is, and who we are to Him. We pray trusting that God knows our limited vision and that sometimes we don't even know what we want or what to ask for.

When we pray to God as our hearts blaze with faith, we entrust ourselves into His care. We pray and trust that God will honor our prayers in His holy judgement, and use His power in our lives to bring us to the final heavenly destination He has prepared for us. Then we wait with holy anticipation, because we never know what God's answer is going to look like in our lives. We ask from our limited perspectives, and God answers from His all-knowing power.

God hears us; our prayers matter to Him. We are never out of God's reach. He lives in each and every Christian—we are His temple. What a marvelous God!

> *To him who is able to keep you from stumbling and to present you before his glorious presence without fault and with great joy—to the only God our Savior be glory, majesty, power and authority, through Jesus Christ our Lord, before all ages, now and forevermore! Amen.* (Jude 24, NIV)

Explore and Exerscise

1. What did your prayers look like in the last week? Check off all those that apply and add your own prayer habit if it is not listed.

   ___ alone
   ___ hands folded/eyes closed
   ___ out loud
   ___ silently in your mind
   ___ in your own words
   ___ in a song
   ___ in an emergency
   ___ with your spouse/friend
   ___ when you woke up
   ___ while driving
   ___ with laughter
   ___ in meditation
   ___ while creating art

   ___ in a group
   ___ kneeling
   ___ whispered
   ___ as part of a liturgy
   ___ without any words
   ___ at meal time
   ___ while in a meeting
   ___ while in a meeting
   ___ before sleeping
   ___ while crying
   ___ on a walk
   ___ while journaling
   ___ other

2. Someone unfamiliar with Christ may ask you, "What is prayer?" How would you answer in a way that they might understand? Be imaginative and craft an answer that doesn't depend on any religious knowledge, vocabulary, or understanding.

3. Read James 5:13-18.

   a. What kinds of answers to prayer does James talk about?

   b. According to James, what place does confession of sins have in prayer?

4. What do our beliefs, faith, and trust in God have to do with prayer? What do you think God does with prayers that begin with "If you can…" or are half-heartedly offered?

5. Read 2 Corinthians 1:3-11.

   a. According to Paul, how important was it that others were praying for him and his companions?

b. Have you experienced others praying over you and for you? Share what this has meant to you.

6. **Prayer Challenge**: Meditation is a prayerful quest for God-engaging thought, imagination, emotion, and desire. If you are unfamiliar with meditative prayer, try this simple method. (It is often helpful to start with a specified amount of time as you learn this practice. Setting a timer helps your mind to not focus on the passage of time instead of God.)

   a. Choose a phrase that you will use to focus your thoughts on God, such as, "Come, Lord Jesus;" "Jesus Christ, Son of the Living God, have mercy on me;" or "The Lord is my Shepherd, I lack for nothing."

   b. Assume a comfortable, relaxed posture; relax your body and mind. Sometimes, it is helpful to do a series of repeated movements, stretches, or exercises first to help your body relax before you assume a comfortable position.

   c. Close your eyes and begin the prayer with the phrase you chose.

      i. Silently repeat your phrase in your heart.

      ii. If you realize your mind has wandered, don't worry. Simply begin repeating your phrase, or some memorized scripture, or the words of a hymn to bring your mind back to God.

      iii. If you feel engulfed by the presence of God, just give yourself over to God's presence.

      iv. At the end of your time of prayer, close with a thank you.

7. **Prayer Challenge.** For some of us, our prayer closet may be our bed. We wake up in the middle of the night and toss and turn while willing ourselves to go back to sleep. We long to rest in God's quiet comfort, but it's impossible because our brains won't turn off. It's time to pray!

> *Only in returning to me and resting in me will you be saved. In quietness and confidence is your strength.* (Isaiah 30:15, NLT)

Praise brings us to rest in God, so try going through the alphabet thinking of attributes of God that begin with A, B, C, etc. Or hymns. Or Bible verses. When we do so, our brain patterns change from focusing on ourselves to God, from anxiety to trust, from stress to resting in the arms of our Heavenly Father.

PART 3: CHAPTER 10

Power Through Prayer

We are in partnership with God;
He makes divine decisions and
implements them through our prayers.

Do you rely on the prayers of other people? Maybe you have trouble concentrating, finding time in your schedule, or successfully practicing daily quiet times. You know others who pray: your parents, your pastors, or your church's resident prayer warriors. It may be time to ask yourself a few questions. Do you let others take your vacation for you? Eat for you? Take your place to walk hand-in-hand with the one you love? Of course not. Then, why would you let prayer be a second-hand experience?

> *Come close to God, and God will come close to you...Humble yourselves before the Lord, and he will lift you up in honor.* (James 4:8a & 10, NLT)

Spending time with God is one of those things that you need to do for yourself. Your prayer life won't look like your spouse's, your neighbor's, or that of your Bible study leader—it is a conversation between you and your Creator. Engaging in prayer with God yourself is an essential part of being in relationship with Him. He is waiting to hear your voice.

God didn't yell at Abraham to get his attention. He simply gave instructions to a man who was listening (Genesis 12). God didn't reach out and grab Moses either, but instead put a burning bush in view that Moses could choose to investigate or not (Exodus 3). God did call Samuel's name in the middle of the night, but despite the temptation to roll over and go right back to sleep, Samuel chose to listen to God's voice (1 Samuel 3). Ananias was praying when he heard God tell him to go minister to Saul, who was a man on a mission to kill followers of The Way. Ananias' first response may very well have been, "God, surely you didn't say 'Saul!'

Tell me I misheard the name!" But he went to see Saul in spite of having every earthly reason to hide from the man (Acts 9).

What did these Biblical people have in common? God was at the center of their lives: they knew Him, trusted His voice, and obeyed. Their relationships weren't formed through occasional visits squeezed into hectic schedules; they made spending time in the presence of God a habitual part of their everyday lives.

WE ARE PRAYER PARTNERS WITH GOD

Even though God is wholly self-sufficient, He designed our relationship with Him to include prayer. He waits for us to pray.

For us, prayer is as essential as breathing. We need to breathe to live: to exhale the dirty, used-up air in our lungs and inhale life-giving oxygen. Prayer provides that same essential pattern of give and take for our spirits: as we exhale our pain, sin, and sorrow, our Good Shepherd powerfully provides all we need as we inhale His goodness.

> *I looked for someone who might rebuild the wall of righteousness that guards the land. I searched for someone to stand in the gap in the wall so I wouldn't have to destroy the land, but I found no one.* (Ezekiel 22:30, NLT)

In Ezekiel, God was yearning to grant mercy to Jerusalem, but not one person was praying for God to spare His people. God has placed Himself in partnership with us, bound Himself to not act without a human intercessor. God set up a system of prayer in which He withholds—judgement, mercy, revival, etc.—unless righteous people pray. In the Bible, God invites, exhorts, and implores us to pray in His name, in His will. Not only that, He promises that any ordinary, sincere, born-again believer can pray and trust that God will answer. Prayer is a part of being in close relationship with God: this is His will and our need. **We are in partnership with God: He makes divine decisions and implements them through our prayers.**

Prayer changes things; it makes a difference for good in this world. Interacting with God, as individuals or in groups, brings

God's power into the battle against evil. In addition, God provides a complete suit of armor for us to wear, to face each day as warriors ready for combat: the belt of truth, the breastplate of righteousness, the feet coverings of readiness, the shield of faith, the helmet of salvation, and the sword of the Spirit (Ephesians 6:14-17). Scriptures show us a sequential pattern—a chain reaction—that readies each piece of armor for us to wear every day.

Don't worry about anything; instead, pray about everything. Tell God what you need, and thank him for all he has done. (Philippians 4:6, NLT)

WE HAVE A HISTORY WITH GOD THAT INCLUDES PRAYER

In God's perfect, intentional will, we were created and placed in the Garden of Eden. It was there that "He walked with us, and He talked with us, and He told us we were His own" in the words of Charles Austin Miles' old hymn. Unlike God's beautiful garden, our sinful world is a war zone. Because of our own choices, both then and now, our sin lays roadblocks and landmines inside us that can separate us from God, but God made a way for us to remain in Him despite our sins (John 3:16-17).

After God brought the Israelites out of slavery in Egypt, they wandered in the desert for forty years. During that time, they were attacked by the Amalekites. Moses instructed his general, Joshua, to lead the fight while he prayed. Moses climbed to the top of a hill above the battlefield and prayed, holding his staff high so that all could see. However, his staff was heavy, and as the day wore on, Moses found himself unable to keep it raised high in the air. Since the Amalekite warriors prevailed when he lowered his staff, Moses sat down, and his companions, Aaron and Hur, held his arms up for him while they continued to pray together until sunset. God answered Moses' persistent prayer with victory (Exodus 17:10-13). Notice that Moses and his friends prayed fervently, but it was God's response and strength that brought the Israelites a victory over the enemy that day.

Elijah didn't have any super powers either, but when he prayed, God unleashed His heavenly power to control the weather.

> *Elijah was a human being, even as we are. He prayed earnestly that it would not rain, and it did not rain on the land for three and a half years. Again he prayed, and the heavens gave rain, and the earth produced its crops.* (James 5:16-18, NIV)

God not only stopped the rain, but when Elijah challenged Baal's prophets, God sent fire down from heaven. Then Elijah prayed for the drought to end, and God sent a wisp of a cloud to signal an oncoming deluge. As an added bonus, He gave Elijah the strength to run in front of the king's chariot all the to Jezreel (1 Kings 18). When Elijah prayed, "the power of the Lord" came upon him and enabled miracles. And afterward, when despair and depression grabbed hold of Elijah, God cared for him and gently reminded him that the God of the Universe was his shepherd.

Jesus prayed for us, all the time; *"My prayer is not for the world, but for those you have given me, because they belong to you"* (John 17:9, NLT). Believers in the early church followed his teaching and made time to pray together a part of every day (Acts 2:42).

Before Jesus went to the cross to die for us, He went to the Garden to pray for us (Luke 22:41). He spoke to His Father about you and me, about our "unfair" world filled with sin and sickness. Full of passionate love, Jesus decided in the Garden that He would rather go to hell than not have you, me, us, with Him in heaven.

It is through the cross that we receive the victories of atonement, access, and inheritance. Jesus wasn't defeated by death and hell, but achieved victory when He rose up from the grave—He's alive (Mark 16:6)! It's hard to imagine a love so wide and deep, but that's the kind of love our Good Shepherd has for us (John 10:11-15).

God's will for us now, in our present earthly circumstances, hasn't changed. He still desires an abiding relationship with us— He has never left us and will never leave us alone. Praise, faith, and prayer bring the power to disable every explosive situation that threatens to detonate and create a breach between us and God. But God promises that we will never be separated from Him (Romans 8:38).

Listen up, believers! Praying for an outflow of God's power did not just happen in ancient stories. **God still answers our prayers with His power today and will do so for all of our tomorrows.**

An important part of conversation is listening, and sometimes we have a hard time distinguishing God's voice among the distractions and worries of life. We get to a quiet place, but our minds speed through a loop of questions and doubts that only lead to more problems and insecurities. When that happens, we might not understand, or even hear, His replies. We are not alone in this issue.

John the Baptist, the man who introduced Jesus to the world, was overwhelmed by doubt when imprisoned in a dark dungeon cell. How did John the Baptizer, the man who had heard the voice of God from heaven say, *"This is my dearly loved Son, who brings me great joy"* (Matthew 3:17, NLT), become John the Doubter? His forced inaction and fear-filled circumstances gave plenty of time for his mind to spin in circles. He had seen Jesus and heard God's voice, but it didn't match up with the picture that he still held in his mind of the Messiah—a Savior who would rescue his people from their earthly problems. John's doubts made him so miserable, he sent his disciples to ask Jesus to explain.

Jesus answered, *"Go back to John and tell him what you have heard and seen—the blind see, the lame walk, those with leprosy are cured, the deaf hear, the dead are raised to life, and the Good News is being preached to the poor"* (Matthew 11:4-5, NLT). In other words, John, needed to take another look at what Jesus was doing. What did God's voice say to him, both in Jesus' spoken words and through the scriptures? Imagine John's abashed smile as he finally figured out that the Messiah wasn't about rescuing the Israelite nation from Roman rule; Jesus was on earth to resolve heavenly issues.

You could call this conversation between John and Jesus a prayer. After all, the dictionary tells us that a conversation involves "an exchange of sentiments, observations, opinions, or ideas." Prayer is a back-and-forth session that includes both talking and listening. Like John the Baptist, we need to ask God to open our ears, eyes, heart, mind, and soul to listen as God answers our prayers.

May the God of hope fill you with all joy and peace as you trust in him, so that you may overflow with hope by the power of the Holy Spirit. (Romans 15:13, NIV)

HEARING THE VOICE OF GOD

God still speaks to us today, through the Scriptures and the conduit of the Holy Spirit who lives in each and every Christ-follower. But God is not going to knock us over the head to get through to us—we have a choice to make, a part to play, and it calls for our daily attention. Of course, the devil loves that our crazy schedules and the tyranny of the urgent keeps us on a fast-spinning hamster wheel. So what are we to do? Here is what God is doing.

Here I am! I stand at the door and knock. If anyone hears my voice and opens the door, I will come in and eat with that person, and they with me. (Revelation 3:20, NIV)

It's up to us to answer that knock, to invite God to our table, and to enjoy a family dinner together—with the bread of life and ever-flowing water as nourishment for our souls.

It is when we persevere in a daily relationship with God, when we faithfully focus on Him, and when our actions reflect our beliefs, that we enter the throne room of God with prayers for power in Jesus' name. God always hears our prayers.

WE HEAR GOD THROUGH SCRIPTURE. For many of us, a Bible is always close to hand, while in some parts of the world, carrying a Bible openly would result in a death sentence. But no matter what our earthly circumstances are, it is important to memorize, paraphrase, recite, or sing His words, and in every possible way hold and ponder them in our hearts and minds. Even with His words in our minds, sometimes, like John the Baptist, we need His help to understand them.

Chapter 10: Power Through Prayer

> *For the word of God is alive and powerful. It is sharper than the sharpest two-edged sword, cutting between soul and spirit, between joint and marrow. It exposes our innermost thoughts and desires.* (Hebrews 4:12, NLT)

WE HEAR GOD IN NATURE. Contrary to what culture may tell you, there is no division between science and God's word. God spoke and the universe and all the laws of nature were created. To learn about the universe is to glimpse the God who made it all (Romans 1:18-20, Psalm 104).

WE HEAR GOD AS WE PRAY. Peter's friends and fellow believers gathered together to pray, and God's response was a dramatic prison rescue (Acts 12). Followers of Jesus' teaching in New Testament times experienced miracles first-hand in response to prayer and fasting (Acts 4:23-31). As they gathered to pray, God's power filled them so that, in spite of the great danger, they boldly continued to spread the gospel message.

Miraculous responses to prayer are still happening today. In the early 2000s, after years of trying, infertility appointments, drugs, medical doctors, a young couple lost hope of ever having a child. They thought they had gone through their "last option," and brought their pain to their pastor. The pastor suggested that they go through the in vitro procedure one more time (the financial cost was very high), but this time, a group would gather weekly to bathe them in prayer. Here's how a brother, we'll call him Tim, tells the story:

> "Every Sunday for three months, a group of up to fourteen people gathered to pray over my brother and sister-in-law, to pray for pregnancy. The week before the in vitro procedure, we were praying for life and life in abundance. It was during this prayer that many of us heard babies crying. Not just one baby, but whimpers from many tiny mouths. Once we finished praying, I immediately ran outside to see if there was someone at the door or something outside, because I heard babies crying and just couldn't believe it. Another man spoke

prophetic words that this couple would have not just one child, but they would have multiple children.

"A few weeks later, we got the news—they were pregnant with triplets. All three healthy babies are now high school students. They were miracle children. Not only that, but a few years later, this couple got pregnant naturally and had another girl. Scientifically, this was supposed to be impossible. This is THE biggest time I've ever witnessed the power of prayer."

WE RECOGNIZE OUR SHEPHERD'S VOICE. As Martin Luther King Jr. sat at his kitchen table in 1956, terrified by the fear of what might happen to him and his family during the Montgomery bus boycott, he said he heard the voice of Jesus promising, "I will be with you." He went forward with his planned protest.

Psychological Anthropologist Tanya Marie Luhrmann's published a study (December 2012, on CNN's Belief Blog), that shows that roughly ten percent of Christians claim to have had an audible experience with God.

> For the last 10 years, I have been doing anthropological and psychological research among experientially oriented evangelicals, the sort of people who seek a personal relationship with God and who expect that God will talk back. For most of them, most of the time, God talks back in a quiet voice they hear inside their minds, or through images that come to mind during prayer. But many of them also reported sensory experiences of God. They say God touched their shoulder, or that He spoke up from the back seat and said, in a way they heard with their ears, that He loved them. Indeed, in 1999, Gallup reported that 23% of all Americans had heard a voice or seen a vision in response to prayer.
> ~ Tanya Marie Luhrmann, http://religion.blogs.cnn.com/2012/12/29/my-take-if-you-hear-god-speak-audibly-you-usually-arent-crazy/

You might hear a voice inside speaking a specific message. Others might "just know" something, and can point to the time they acquired this knowledge. Someone else might have a name pop into their head out of nowhere, then realize that "nowhere" was actually the Holy Spirit's leading.

GOD SENDS HIS ANGELS. Even Hollywood acknowledges that angels visit humans on earth—although usually portrayed outside of Christian beliefs—in movies such as "It's a Wonderful Life" and television shows like "Touched by an Angel." Our music is also full of angels: In his 1990 book, *Angels: An Endangered Species*, Malcolm Godwin estimates that over the prior 30 years one in every ten pop songs mentioned an angel.

As we know, imitating things of God is a favorite method the devil uses to draw us away from the reality of who and what God is. Believers need to be discerning. The Bible tells us about angels in the context of their actions on God's behalf and for the purpose of informing us further about God, what He does, and how He does it.

In Bible stories, the first things angels say to people is, "Do not be afraid." There must be something very powerful and frightening about angels that necessitates that opening line. Angels are the Lord's messengers, and our reaction should be to listen for God's message and react accordingly. The poem below urges you to make this a personal question.

If an angel appeared to me—
    Not a roly-poly Cupid,
    But a Michael or a Gabriel—
    And told me,
"The Living God had been born on earth,
    He had died here and defeated death for me.
    His Father has sent the Holy Spirit to be with me
    Here, on earth, until He comes again,"
Would I laugh while eavesdropping in her tent like elderly Sarah,
    Ask, "Where'd you get your facts?" like Zechariah to the angel who appeared in his field,
    Answer, "How?" but believe and obey like Mary and Joseph,
    Or run to the nearest stable like the shepherds who had winessed the angel choir?

If an angel told me,
  "A Revival will start here,
  And it will begin with you,"
  Would there have to be vast changes in my life?
If an angel told me,
  "Satan will send his hosts to hurt, defile, ridicule, persecute, slander, and defeat you.
  But don't be afraid.
  God has sent the Heavenly Hosts to battle the dragon."
Would I say,
  "Not me, Lord,
  I'm not the one you need," or
  "Here's what I had in mind to do for you?"
Would I need to touch Your wounds like doubting Thomas,
  Or will I hear Your Biblical message,
  Listen to Your still, small voice,
  Thank the angel for Your message, and obey?
The Gospel of Christ:
  In my mind.
  In my heart.
  On my lips.

> ~ "If an Angel" by Kathleen Evenhouse, December 1995

IN COMMUNITY. God places us in community, and sometimes His message for us comes through those around us, as it did in Tim's story about miraculous pregnancy. The book you are reading is a result of community listening to God together: one person had a vision to share, another felt a calling to write, and another was willing to share his skills in support and encouragement. **Sometimes God's voice is heard in the undercurrent of simple conversation and sometimes takes years of determined obedience.**

VISIONS, DREAMS, AND PROPHECY. Dr. Mark Virkler of "Communion with God Ministries" tells his story of hearing God in his book The 4 Keys to Hearing God's Voice. In the eleven years he had been a pastor, he believed he had never heard the voice of God, and he was frustrated. He prayed about and wrestled with what he thought of as his inability, until one night the Holy Spirit woke him out of a deep sleep with a text reference: Habakkuk 2:1-2. As he pondered this passage, he realized it gave him, and everyone else, the way to hear what God was saying to them: "(1) be still and listen, (2) focus your eyes on God, (3) recognize the spontaneous flow of the Holy Spirit, and (4) write down what you see and hear." As he practiced this method of listening, Dr. Virkler heard God speaking to him, and you can too.

Scripture tells us that we all have eyes, ears, minds, wills, and emotions of our "heart" that need to be attuned to the Holy Spirit in the unique way in which we are designed by God to hear Him. When we do so, each of us can "hear" the Lord's voice. And we must test what we hear: (1) Does it line up with scripture? (2) Ask other trusted Christians to see if what you hear matches up with Biblical teaching. (3) Does the message you heard flow with the fruits of the Holy Spirit?

Many of us who have read the Old Testament may picture a prophet as a bearded hermit dressed in a robe who barges into a situation and thunders that "doom and gloom will come from God unless you people change your ways." His message came from God and was accurate, but it wasn't the whole picture, because God was calling for them to repent and be saved.

A prophet is simply someone who is speaking a message from God that is intended for a particular circumstance or time. It is forth-telling, looking into the future. A prophet is given the ability to see things that others cannot see. She does not focus on the circumstances, but on the God who rules the circumstances; not on the mess of today, but on the solution that God will provide down the road (Acts 2:17-18).

The exciting truth is that prophecy is a spiritual gift that is given for the benefit of all believers (1 Corinthians 12). God wants those to whom He has given the prophetic gift to use it to strengthen, encourage, and comfort others (1 Corinthians 14:1-3). Do you know the Bible message? Can you teach it to others? Then, when you spread the Good News of salvation, you are acting as a prophet.

And afterward, I will pour out my Spirit on all people. Your sons and daughters will prophesy, your old men will dream dreams, your young men will see visions. (Joel 2:28, NIV)

As we interact with Jesus through prayer, praise, and scripture, the Holy Spirit writes truths on our hearts. This is how God shows us His character and gives us wisdom to apply in our everyday lives. We will hear His voice and sense His direction by encountering Him in His Word.

Do not stifle the Holy Spirit. Do not scoff at prophecies, but test everything that is said. Hold on to what is good. (1 Thessalonians 5:19-21, NLT)

TRUST, PRAY, AND OBEY

Merriam-Webster dictionary defines trust as "an assured reliance on the character, ability, strength, or truth of someone or something." **Our prayer-conversations are built on a foundation of an abiding trust in God.**

What if our churches were safe harbors of prayer, communities that deeply anchored all who enter even in the storms of life? What if our Christian communities embraced the ministries of healing? What if we were committed to fostering life change through healing ministries of worship, teaching, prayer, and counseling in Christian communities that address the spiritual, physical, mental, and emotional needs of all who trust in His Name?

The early church (Book of Acts) survived opposition and perscution, but no matter what evil brought, it couldn't stop the flow of the gospel. Miracles of healing and rescue—powered by prayers in the name of Jesus—were the doorway many needy people passed through that prepared them to accept the gospel message.

Jesus calls us today to hear His voice, trust in Him, live, and love in the same way as the early Christians did—to be His church. Scripture gives us a clear picture of what The Church should look like:

> *The Spirit of the Sovereign Lord is upon me, for the Lord has anointed me to bring good news to the poor, has sent me to comfort the brokenhearted, and to proclaim that captives will be released and prisoners will be freed.* (Isaiah 61:1-2, NLT)
>
> *He [Jesus] gave them power and authority to cast out all demons and to heal all diseases.* (Luke 9:1, NLT)
>
> *For where two or three gather together as my followers, I am there among them."* (Matthew 18:20, NLT)
>
> *I pray that out of his glorious riches he may strengthen you with power through his Spirit in your inner being, so that Christ may dwell in your hearts through faith. And I pray that you, being rooted and established in love, may have power, together with all the Lord's holy people, to grasp how wide and long and high and deep is the love of Christ, and to know this love that surpasses knowledge—that you may be filled to the measure of all the fullness of God.* (Ephesians 3:15-19, NIV)
>
> *Keep on asking, and you will receive what you ask for. Keep on seeking, and you will find. Keep on knocking, and the door will be opened to you. For everyone who asks, receives. Everyone who seeks, finds. And to everyone who knocks, the door will be opened. "You parents—if your children ask for a loaf of bread, do you give them a stone instead? Or if they ask for a fish, do you give them a snake? Of course not! So if you sinful people know how to give good gifts to your children, how much more will your heavenly Father give good gifts to those who ask him?* (Matthew 7:7-11, NLT)

Our prayers undergird our actions with His strength, and that makes a difference. When the fruits of the Spirit (founded in *agapé* love) flow through us, people are attracted to the church in the same way that moths are drawn to a light source. As our relationship with God grows, Holy Spirit initiated, fruit-filled lives draw the needy and the curious, giving us opportunities to boldly proclaim the gospel message (Galatians 5:22-23).

What is our responsibility in this unleashing of God's power? Be persistent in prayer! Moses' battlefield prayer, with assistance from his fellow believers, was a whole-day marathon. Elijah's prayers were uttered over a course of years—years where he experienced evil on all sides including the murder of fellow prophets. **But he held onto his faith, trusted his God, and continued to pray.**

> *Is anyone among you in trouble? Let them pray. Is anyone happy? Let them sing songs of praise. Is anyone among you sick? Let them call the elders of the church to pray over them and anoint them with oil in the name of the Lord. And the prayer offered in faith will make the sick person well; the Lord will raise them up. If they have sinned, they will be forgiven. Therefore, confess your sins to each other and pray for each other so that you may be healed. The prayer of a righteous person is powerful and effective.* (James 5:13-16, NIV)

Chain Reaction of Praise

The next sequence that follows prayer in our chain reaction is "overcoming evil." It flows out of prayers that include speaking, listening, and stepping out in obedience. Our participation with God through prayer helps to bring "His Kingdom to earth as it is in heaven."

- Sarah was barren and far too old to bear a child, but in faith, she believed God's promise and gave birth to Isaac (Genesis 18:9-15, 21:1-2).

- Hannah's tearful prayers weren't even intelligible to human ears, but she believed God's promise from Eli's mouth, and this barren woman returned home to prepare for a child (1 Samuel 1).

These women were not super heroes, but like Moses and Elijah they prayed, listened, believed, and in obedient faith stepped into God's Kingdom on earth.

God rocked their world.

When we participate in faithful prayer, His strength makes all the difference. God wants to hear from you. We can't continue life as we have always lived it, but instead choose to grow new dimensions in our relationship with the Almighty God. Sacrifice the old ways to make room for the new—take the risk, make the plunge. Take it to God in prayer.

God will rock your life too.

Explore and Exercise

1. In Medieval times, safety was pictured as a castle surrounded by a moat. During the Cold War era, security may have been a well-stocked bomb shelter buried deep in your backyard. Today, we rely on satellites, drones, and smart bombs.

    Identify an earthly haven(s) that you tend to turn to or that may make you feel secure.

2. "Ascending into God's Heavenly Throne Room" is a phrase that Christians may use to express having open access to God. A human equivalent to this might be the opportunity to step through the door of the Oval Office in the White House any time day or night: to come in, make yourself comfortable, and chat with the most powerful person in the country about whatever is on your mind. However, it's nowhere near equivalent. With God, you don't have to try to secure an empty slot in a crowded calendar, pass through any security checks, or meet any qualifications. God has given us a "Get in Free" card.

    a. What does free access to God's throne room tell us about how our relationship with God?

    b. If you were invited to consult every day with someone you considered to be the wisest person alive, how would you take advantage of it? So, how are you responding to God's invitation?

    c. What do we acknowledge when we praise God? Share why you think praise might be considered our access key to the throne room?

3. Explain why God wants us to participate in this conversation with God called prayer?

4. Read James 4:1-10 in The Message:

    ¹⁻² *Where do you think all these appalling wars and quarrels come from? Do you think they just happen? Think again. They come about*

because you want your own way, and fight for it deep inside yourselves. You lust for what you don't have and are willing to kill to get it. You want what isn't yours and will risk violence to get your hands on it.

²⁻³ You wouldn't think of just asking God for it, would you? And why not? Because you know you'd be asking for what you have no right to. You're spoiled children, each wanting your own way.

⁴⁻⁶ You're cheating on God. If all you want is your own way, flirting with the world every chance you get, you end up enemies of God and his way. And do you suppose God doesn't care? The proverb has it that "he's a fiercely jealous lover." And what he gives in love is far better than anything else you'll find. It's common knowledge that "God goes against the willful proud; God gives grace to the willing humble."

⁷⁻¹⁰ So let God work his will in you. Yell a loud no to the Devil and watch him scamper. Say a quiet yes to God and he'll be there in no time. Quit dabbling in sin. Purify your inner life. Quit playing the field. Hit bottom, and cry your eyes out. The fun and games are over. Get serious, really serious. Get down on your knees before the Master; it's the only way you'll get on your feet. (James 4:1-10)

    a. What does your obedience in engaging in conversation with God (in prayer) tell you about yourself? About your desires? About God?

    b. If God knows everything and is in control of all that happens, why do you think He invites us to pray? Why would our participation make a difference?

5. Share a time when you heard from God.

    a. What were the circumstances?

    b. In what way did you hear God's voice?

    c. Do you actively listen for God's voice? Explain how you do this.

6. A well-known but uncredited quote is: "There are no atheists in foxholes." This is most often used to express the speaker's

belief that all people seek a divine power when they are facing an extreme threat. Have you spent some time "in foxholes" during your life? How do these experiences affect your relationship and attachment to God?

7. **Prayer Challenge**: Physical movement can help us move into a quiet time with God. Many of us already use physical cues, such as folding our hands and closing our eyes, when we prepare to pray. These physical movements act as a trigger—in our minds, bodies, and souls—to bring us more fully into God's presence.

   The point of the exercise regiment demonstrated below is to help each of us find a way to quiet our minds in order to hear God. Figure out what works for you and make that your daily habit.

   a. Softly play an instrumental sound track with a steady, quiet beat.

   b. Spend a few (5 to 7) minutes engaging in slow, sustained, repetitive motions that engage the entire body. These mostion should be simple, easy to follow, and not require special skills or strength levels. (Aternatively, walk briskly, dance to a favorite praise song, or do another sort of physical movement that gets your whole body and mind working together.) The idea is to get your mind, body, and soul synchorized as one unit.

   c. Find a comfortable position in a chair with hands (palms open to ceiling) resting on their thighs. You could also lie down on a mat or bed on your back. Use deep breaths, blowing them out slowly as you move into a comfortable position, concentrating on relaxing your head, your face, your neck, your shoulders, all the way down to your toes to relax each part of your body.

   d. Begin regular, slow breathing focusing on God by breathing His name, praising Him, or just saying, "Hello, God. I'm so glad to be with you today." If your to-do list starts to intrude or worries fill your mind, go back to deep breaths, thinking your welcome phrase as you exhale.

    e. While the music continues, spend about four minutes in quiet, personal time with God.

8. **Prayer Challenge**: What new way, new dimension, or new habits are you willing to take on in order for God to do something new in your life? Go to God in prayer and ask Him to show you how to deepen your relationship with Him. Write down what that will look like and commit yourself to risk making this change in your life for a month. Ask the Holy Spirit for strength and persistence.

PART 4

Overcome Evil

It takes exercise to grow our faith and basic combat training to overcome evil.

[Jesus said,] But the time is coming—indeed it's here now—when you will be scattered, each one going his own way, leaving me alone. Yet I am not alone because the Father is with me. I have told you all this so that you may have peace in me. Here on earth you will have many trials and sorrows. But take heart, because I have overcome the world." (John 16:32-33, NLT)

WELCOME TO BASIC TRAINING

The final victory is already won: Jesus paid for our sins, overcame death, and gave us the undeserved gift of salvation. Yet, while we live in this world, we will engage in a battle between good and evil every day. Jesus told the disciples, and He tells us, "Don't be afraid. You are not alone." Indeed, we are armed for battle, and our source of power is God through the Holy Spirit who lives in us.

God doesn't grant His power when we recite religious prayers in a precise manner, like a magical incantation. Instead, God works through relationship with us. He has shown us in His word how to become active members of the Kingdom of God on earth—through a chain reaction that begins with focusing on Him (with praise) in order to light the fires of our faith. When we pray full of trust in Him alone, God releases His power into the world, and we are warriors who can overcome evil.

It takes exercise to grow our faith and basic combat training to overcome evil. Reading or watching videos about it won't equip us for the battle. We can't overcome evil from the bleacher seats—we need to enter the arena. So, filled with the Spirit, put on the armor of God and jump into action in faith and power.

PART 4: CHAPTER 11

Story Time: Past and Present

overcome evil

Jonathan, a man of faith, asked God for a sign and received it.

ON HIS OWN, BUT NOT ALONE

An Old Testament Story of Battling Evil: 1 Samuel 13-14

Israel's first king was a tall, handsome man named Saul from the tribe of Benjamin. His story is usually told in connection with David, who eventually succeeded Saul as king. But this is not that story.

This is the story that compares King Saul to his son Jonathan before David came on the scene. Jonathan was a general of one-third of the Israelite army and was greatly feared by the Philistines because of his victories over them. These victories were credited to (his father Saul) the King (I Samuel 18:7), but this story is also not about a brave general who didn't get credit for his army's successes—that was not an issue for Jonathan. It's about two men facing insurmountable odds (humanly speaking) and how they responded differently to the fear that filled them and their troops.

~ ~ ~

King Saul's standing army consisted of three units of trained solders, both Israelites and mercenaries. When the Philistines threatened all-out war, Saul stationed two companies (2,000 men) with him in the hill country of Bethel. Jonathan commanded the third company (1,000 men) that was stationed at Gibeah in Benjamin.

JONATHAN ATTACKED AND DEFEATED the Philistine garrison at Geba, killing the governor stationed there. Mad as hornets at the Israelite revolt, the Philistines rallied their forces to fight Israel: three companies of chariots, six companies of cavalry, and so many infantry they looked like sand on the seashore. This massive army went up into the hills and set up a base camp at Micmash, south of Beth-Aven.

Saul commanded that the rams' horns be blown throughout the kingdom, signaling all the able men (who were trained as local militia) to report for army, joining the king and his troops at Gilgal.

But the Philistines sent out three detachments of raiding parties from their main camp with orders to scout, harass, and rout any Israelite fighters they might come across. And the harassment worked. When the Israelite volunteer soldiers saw the massive presence of ruthless Philistines, many of them panicked and hid rather than making their way past the enemy to join Saul's army. Some were so afraid, they crossed the Jordan River to escape the enemy and watch the battle—intending to join Saul if Israelite triumph was assured or to escape back home in case of a Philistine victory.

> Historical note: The best-armed Israelite soldiers, most of those in the standing army, had bronze weapons. The volunteer militia came with whatever implements they used on their farms, such as knives, axes, and sickles, edged with blades of bronze, sharpened stone, or bone. The Israelites had no chariots or cavalry. Many of their foot soldiers were armed only with slingshots, and these men were employed in battle similar to Philistine archers.
>
> Because of Philistine suppression, there were no blacksmiths in Israel. When they weren't at war, Israelites had to journey into Philistine territory to keep their farm tools sharp and in good repair: at a price of a silver coin for the plowshares and mattocks and half that for other tools. So, when the battle of Micmash began, there wasn't an iron sword or spear-tip to be found anywhere in Israel—except those wielded by Saul and his son Jonathan (Samuel 13:19-22).

SAUL and his standing troops REMAINED HIDDEN in their caves at Gilgal, WAITING ANXIOUSLY for word from the Lord from the prophet Samuel who was scheduled to arrive within seven days. As the days passed, fear overcame faith and courage, so much so that even some of Saul's battle-hardened soldiers deserted and hid in the surrounding wilderness.

AFRAID AND UNWILLING TO WAIT for God's word through His prophet, SAUL defied the system God had set up through Moses and decided to serve as a priest himself by burning offerings on the altar. The prophet, Samuel, arrived just as Saul had done this and asked, "What on earth are you doing?"

"You didn't come when you said you were," SAUL ACCUSED the prophet. "Haven't you seen the size of the Philistine army and the damage they've done. Look at the state of my army! I had to do something, SO I TOOK MATTERS INTO MY OWN HANDS."

"How foolish you have been, Saul! If you had done as your God commanded since the time that God told me to anoint you as king, by now God would have set a firm and lasting foundation under your rule over Israel. But look around you; your kingly rule is already falling to pieces. God is out looking for your replacement right now. Your kingdom must end." With those words, Samuel left the camp.

Saul went out to meet the Philistines with the army he had left—when he counted there were only 600 soldiers. He set up battle camp under a pomegranate tree on the outskirts of Gibeah, south of the pass, while the Philistine army was encamped on the north side. But SAUL, STILL FULL OF FEAR AND DESPERATE to rally his troops, continued to usurp God's authority and power. Rather than turning to God ask forgiveness and help, Saul assigned priestly duties to Abijah, whose family's sins had caused them to be excluded from the priesthood.

JONATHAN snuck out of the camp without telling his father. "Come with me to CHECK OUT THE PHILISTINE GARRISON on the other side of the pass," he said to his armor bearer, who was also his apprentice and loyal friend.

The Philistine outpost was on top of a steep cliff faced with rocky outcroppings, sand, and thorn bushes. From the opposite cliff, Jonathan considered their options—the two men would have to make their way across the pass and climb the opposite cliff. A seasoned commander, Jonathan knew not to attack from a lower position, not to let the enemy know you are coming, and not to attack against overwhelming odds with no backup. However, what he suggested to his friend was not dependent on military strategy.

> *"Come on now, let's go across to these uncircumcised pagans. Maybe God will work for us. There's no rule that says God can only deliver by using a big army. No one can stop God from saving when he sets his mind to it."* (1 Samuel 14:6, MSG)

Without hesitation or complaint (or an iron weapon), the young man replied, "Go ahead. Do what you think best. I'm with you all the way." So Jonathan laid out his plan.

> *"Here's what we'll do. We'll cross over the pass and let the men see we're there. If they say, 'Halt! Don't move until we check you out,' we'll stay put and not go up. But if they say, 'Come on up,' we'll go right up—and we'll know God has given them to us. That will be our sign."* (1 Samuel 14:8-10, MSG)

The two men started their climb while Philistine guards responded with taunts. "Looky here. The Hebrew rabbits are finally crawling out of their hidey holes." Others laughed and called out, "Come on up here! We've got a thing or two to show you!"

That was the sign from God that Jonathan had asked for. This young man wasn't filled with battle lust, but was acting as a MAN OF FAITH who had ASKED GOD FOR A SIGN and received it.

"Up! Follow me! THE LORD HAS GIVEN THEM INTO OUR HANDS!" Jonathan shouted as he clambered up the hill on all fours with his apprentice close behind. As they crested the cliff, the Philistines ran at them with terrible war cries and flashing swords, but Jonathan knocked them flat with his sword, and his armor-bearer finished them off, bashing their heads with stones or using the enemy's own weapons against them. On that small cliff-top area, measuring about a half-acre, Jonathan and his apprentice killed about twenty men.

Suddenly, panic broke out in the Philistine army, both in the camp and in the field, including even the outposts and raiding parties.

At the same time, an earthquake struck, and everyone was terrified (1 Samuel 14:15, NLT).

Saul's sentries posted near the pass raced back to tell Saul about the confusion in the Philistine camp.

> *Saul commanded, "Line up and take the roll. See who's here and who's missing." When they called the roll, Jonathan and his armor bearer turned up missing.* (1 Samuel 14:17, MSG)

Saul ordered his pseudo-priest to see what God had to say, but the upheaval in the Philistine camp became greater and louder. SO SAUL ABANDONED HIS PLAN TO SEEK GOD. Instead, he called his army together, and they went straight to the battle. At the Philistine base camp they found total confusion—Philistines were swinging their swords wildly, killing each other. The timid Israelite militiamen who had hidden earlier and those who had defected hurried to join their countrymen when they saw the Philistines running away.

FRIGHTENED, SAUL DEPENDED ON HIS OWN PLANS at the head of a fearful army unwilling to fight.

IN FAITH, JONATHAN FOLLOWED GOD'S LEADING to jump into the arena, and God granted victory.

"KENNY, I'M HERE."

A Modern-Day True Story: A Call to Be Ready

"It was like any early morning at work," Kenny said. "I walked around the church facility checking a few things before I started on the day's to-do list."

Kenny is one of four people who manage the cleaning, care, set-up, and maintenance of the church property, facilities, and campus. He's a behind-the-scenes person who works to make things run smoothly, and that's how he likes it.

"I went through the closed doors of the sanctuary and started walking down the aisle toward the front of the sanctuary to check a big fan that was drying out the carpet after a small leak." Kenny shrugged his soldiers. "It was just a normal day, a normal job."

"Kenny, I'm here," a voice said.

Kenny stopped walking. "Who's here?" Kenny asked. He hadn't seen anyone else in the building.

"I am Michael," the voice answered.

Turning slowly, Kenny stared at a very bright bluish light where nothing had been seconds before. His first reaction was surprised confusion, until the words sunk in, "I am Michael."

"It's an angel," Kenny's mind yelled at him. "And he's talking to me."

Backing up, Kenny sat down hard on the nearest seat, shocked, amazed, and very much in awe of the strong presence in the room. And then Michael was gone.

"I don't think I even remembered to check the fan," Kenny said. "I was in shock. I didn't know very much about angels, and it had never occurred to me that I might see one."

Kenny hurried to tell the pastor what had just happened and learned that Michael was a very important angel, the leader of the angel armies.

"The Archangel Michael called me by name," months later Kenny's voice was still filled with awe. "He knew who I was, and He wanted me to understand that he was there."

Since that encounter, Kenny's been studying to learn more about angels and visions. "Archangel Michael is a protector and the leader of the army of God against the forces of evil; he's the angel that battled his way through the Persian evil spirits to bring God's message to Daniel. I still have no idea why Michael picked me to see him," Kenny said. "I believe that somehow our church needs to be prepared for some kind of big battle that is coming—that's why Michael was here."

"What I know for sure is this: God wants soldiers willing to battle against evil," Kenny said. "And I'm ready."

Chapter 11: Story Time, Past and Present 153

Like Gideon in Judges 6, Kenny was just going about life as usual, doing the day's work, when they both were interrupted by an unexpected visitor. Gideon was given a task, but Michael didn't give Kenny clear instructions. Even though Kenny doesn't know when and where he will be called to fight, he's not just sitting around. He is readying himself by walking closely with God, preparing for whatever battle the Lord has in store for him.

Explore and Exercise

1. Jonathan was prompted by God to act, an action that the rest of the troops—even his father, Saul,—would have called crazy (1 Samuel 14). Jonathan's friend came with him. We are not told his name, but he recognized Jonathan's faith in God and followed him into battle without question.

    a. If you were the one accompanying Jonathan on his scouting mission, what would it take to convince you to follow him up the ridge to battle superior forces?

    b. Compare Saul's and Jonathan's actions as they prepared to engage the enemy. Look for words in the text that give you clues about their faith and general attitude. How did God make His power evident in this story?

    c. Share a time you were called to something which could be considered unwise from a human perspective. How did you respond? Did faith affect your decision and your actions?

2. Have you ever experienced a heavenly message (voice, knowledge, or vision) or encountered a heavenly messenger? As you share this with your group, remember this activity is not intended as a competition with others, but to encourage each other. Each one of us hears from God in unique ways, and **everyone can hear from Him**. Focus on the One who knocks on the door of your heart and learn to recognize His special rhythmic knock to which you respond.

    a. Share a time that you may have wondered, "Was that a coincidence or was that God? As you think back through the situation, what conclusions do you come to?

    b. Look back at your last week to identify the issues or people that were on your mind. Perhaps one way you overcame evil involved moving from anxious thoughts to prayer. Share a "God sighting" that you have experienced in response to your prayers.

3. **Overcoming Evil Challenge: Believe that God is Actively helping you OVERCOME EVIL in your life.** The following idea has been promoted by many over the years: When we look at a painting and try to understand its meaning, each of us sees only what we are prepared to understand through the filters of our own bias and experiences. Stated simply, "we see what we are looking for." For example, if a face reminds you of someone with whom you have had a bad experience, you might have a negative reaction to the new person. Your adoration or hate depends on who the viewer is reminded of.

   Scientific experiments have shown that what we think we see is often affected by what we expect to see. But the Bible tells us that **we can choose to see differently**—through faith vision—and challenge the devil in God's power. The verses below offer a few examples of actions based on this new mindset.

   > *Don't forget to show hospitality to strangers, for some who have done this have entertained angels without realizing it!* (Hebrews 13:2, NLT)

   > *Isn't it obvious that all angels are sent to help out with those lined up to receive salvation?* (Hebrews 1:14, MSG)

   Our perception comes out of what we believe, out of our faith and trust in the Almighty God. In order for us to overcome evil, we must walk in close relation with Him—God is as real and as close to us as a person holding our hand.

   a. Discuss why you agree or disagree with the premise stated above: "we see what we are looking for." How could this apply to our belief in God and our relationship with Him? In other words, do you have to believe that God speaks to you today to recognize a message or messenger from Him when it's put in front of you?

   b. There are times in your life when you may find it difficult to see or hear God, *no matter how hard you try.*

      i. Reread the sentence above (b) focusing on the italicized words. Does this ring true to you? If not, why not?

ii. Take a moment to talk about the circumstances, doubts, stressors, or fears that may be prevent us from hearing God's voice or seeing His hand in our everyday lives.

c. The Chain Reaction starts with (1) praise which lights the fire of (2) faith. Communicating with God in prayer is Step #3. Why do you think (4) overcoming evil is fourth in the list?

Chain Reaction of Praise

PART 4: CHAPTER 12

At War with Evil

You cannot straddle the thin line
between good and evil.
You have to fight to conquer,
or you will be conquered.

Colossians 3:10 sums up our purpose and states the focus of our lives very clearly: Put on your new nature, and be renewed as you learn to know your Creator and become like him. This is how we receive the strength and authority to overcome evil: to follow so closely in His footsteps that we become dust-covered disciples in the process of transforming our character into that of our rabbi. It is in this kind of attachment to God that we are renewed day by day (2 Corinthians 4:16). The process began when we accepted God's invitation to step into His Circle of Love; we were immersed in a chain reaction in which each state of being initiates the next:

> Strike a match of PRAISE in all circumstances,
>
> To light the fire of FAITH that God has given you,
>
> And God will answer your PRAYERS
> in His great power, timing, and will,
>
> So that you can OVERCOME EVIL in this world.
>
> In this relationship. we REIGN and RULE with Christ
> on Earth and for Eternity.

Overcoming evil is not a fly-by-the-seat-of-your-pants activity. It takes spiritual exercise, training, and dogged persistence as we choose to live in close relationship with God—a heavenly goal built on daily choice. And God grants us the power to overcome evil, to declare—speak out loud—against evil presence with God's authority (Ephesians 1:19-20).

OVERCOME OR BE OVERCOME

Jesus sent 70 disciples traveling from town-to-town to spread the gospel message (Luke 10). He told them, "Take nothing with you," because God would provide. He warned them of danger, "you will be lambs in a wolf pack," and although they carried no physical weapons, they were well-armed to overcome evil. In Jesus' name they performed miraculous healings, which in turn, gave them opportunity to spread the gospel to a wide audience.

The disciples came back to Jesus crowing with excitement and reported that even the demons had obeyed them. Jesus smiled and said, "Of course they did. I personally witnessed Satan being thrown out of heaven; in fact, I threw him out. I have placed this same authority and power over evil in your hands. But here's what you should be really excited about: not your authority over evil, but that God's authority is with you and, also, present in you. See, it's not what you do for God, it's what God does for you—that's the reason to dance and sing for joy!" (Luke 11:18-19)

Jesus gave the disciples clear legal authority to fight the war against evil, to take offensive action in the conflict with the devil (Matthew 28:18-20). There were no legal loopholes that disqualified the disciples. We, the church, also have a legal grounding for our battle against evil in order to be the controlling factor in human affairs. It is God's intention that we militantly walk in the Spirit as overcomers in the same authority, power, and divine presence as Jesus walked (John 20:21).

Do not be overcome by evil, but overcome evil with good. (Romans 12:21, NIV)

This verse seems to give us a choice between two things—good and evil—and tells us which one we should choose. You cannot straddle the thin line between the two; you have to fight to conquer, or you will be conquered. There will not be a peace treaty, a truce, or a suspension of hostilities. God calls us to overcome evil, and because He tells us to do it, we know it is possible.

As His dust-covered disciples, God doesn't limit our divine resources (Ephesians 3:19), but gives us everything that we need to join the battle. Be joyful, God has given us the keys to the Kingdom. At the same time, God doesn't compel us to use them. He patiently waits, and the rest is up to us.

If it had been God's will to do so, Satan would have been thrown into the lake of fire already rather than at the end of the age (Revelation 20:10). His defeat is a surety, but not yet. Evidently, God sees an ongoing role for Satan that is essential for His purposes in the world. This world is a training ground for believers; this is where we learn how to reign and rule with Christ for eternity. The battle to establish God's Kingdom "on earth as it is in heaven" is a boot camp that trains us to be overcomers, to use the weapons of praise and faith, to pray powerful prayers to overcome evil, and to enforce Christ's victory that He so dearly bought.

The Bible tells us of Satan's plots and Christ's ultimate victory:

> *Whoever makes a practice of sinning is of the devil, for the devil has been sinning from the beginning. The reason the Son of God appeared was to destroy the works of the devil.* (1 John 3:8, MSG)
>
> *Because God's children are human beings—made of flesh and blood—the Son also became flesh and blood. For only as a human being could he die, and only by dying could he break the power of the devil, who had the power of death.* (Hebrews 2:14, NLT)
>
> *In this way, he [Jesus] disarmed the spiritual rulers and authorities. He shamed them publicly by his victory over them on the cross.* (Colossians 2:15, NLT)

Who exactly is it that we are fighting? The Bible tells us that the devil is a liar and the father of lies (John 8:44). On his first appearance in the Bible (Genesis 3) he twists the truth (Did God say, 'You shall not eat of any tree in the garden?'), and follows it up with a subtle lie (You will not die). Peter tells us the devil prowls around like hungry lion looking for lunch (1 Peter 5:8), that he has blinded the minds of believers ((2 Corinthians 4:4), and that he is a very cunning deceiver (2 Corinthians 11:3). The devil even disguises himself as an angel of light and his misguided minions as servants of righteousness (2 Corinthians 11:13-15). Satan's undertaking is to choke off the faith of God's people, and so he builds roadblocks and firewalls in our inner beings of fear, busyness, false guilt, feelings of worthlessness, and apathy, among many others.

In this world, we will have trouble (John 16:33). One of the most sobering facts about life is that all humans have a supernatural enemy whose aim is to use pain and pleasure to make us blind, stupid, and miserable—forever. Scripture names him: the devil and Satan, the deceiver of the whole world...the accuser (Revelation 12:9–10), the ruler of this world (John 12:31), and the god of this age (2 Corinthians 4:4).

But we don't have to be afraid. God is sovereign over Satan. "Good warfare" is the term Scripture uses to describe our earthly battles against hell (1 Timothy 1:18) despite our suffering and possible death (Revelation 2:10). Satan loves to twist God's words to cause us to wonder how God can use "good" and" war" to describe each other. This war is good because it is in the fighting that we refine our faith. It is good because God is our great general in combat, and He communicates with us constantly using the walkie-talkie of prayer. He knows the enemy's strategies and passes his evil designs on to us so that we won't be outwitted by Satan (2 Corinthians 2:11).

You see, Satan can entice someone to sin, but he cannot force us to do so. God has given us the ability to choose and supplies His power to enable us to choose to follow Him (Philippians 2:13). Satan cannot recapture that person who is "in Christ." **Therefore, Satan is a defeated enemy, one who ultimately will be thrown into the lake of fire.** However, until that time, he is still very active in our world. Even so, God gives us clear direction on **how to deal the devil a decisive blow—hold fast to Christ.**

Despite what the devil would like us to believe, Satan does not have a free hand in this world. He is on a leash so that he can do no more than God permits. In fact, he even must get heavenly permission. In Luke 22, Jesus told Simon Peter that Satan had asked to have complete freedom over Peter in order to "sift this disciple like wheat." In the case of Job, Satan asked God's council to stop their protection of this righteous man, to let Satan ruin his life because then he would surely curse God's name. God answered, *"Behold, Job is in your hands, only spare his life"* (Job 2:6). Both Job and Peter chose to hold fast to Christ.

Satan knows what Christ did to him at Calvary and through His resurrection, but he desperately carries on guerilla warfare to gain power over us using subterfuge, deception, and bluff. It is when we forget who we are that we can be distracted by demons of fear, sickness, disease, or limitations of any kind. Remember, believers, we are in Christ, and as Satan cannot touch Christ, he cannot touch us. Rejoice, Christians, and praise God! We are risen and exalted with Christ, united with Him on the throne with all enemies under His feet.

God could have already put Satan away, but He has chosen instead to use him to give the Church a boot camp experience, a training ground, an apprenticeship in which we learn how to fight the good fight and practice overcoming evil. The crown belongs to the conqueror, and the victory has already been won.

THE WAR IS FOUGHT ON TWO FRONTS

Your hand-to-hand combat is not with human beings, but with the highest principalities and authorities operating in rebellion under the heavenly realms. For they are a powerful class of demon-gods and evil spirits that hold this dark world in bondage. (Ephesians 6:12, TPT)

Many of us have a hard time acknowledging or comprehending spiritual warfare. We'd rather close our eyes and pretend that if we refuse to fight the war is not real, but the fight is on.

WE FIGHT TO OVERCOME EVIL ON EARTH. The war is inside, outside, and all around us (Romans 7:14-25). Each one of us is, by nature, sinful. We have the desire to do good, but can't carry it out. When we want to do good, evil is right there fighting us. The war between good and evil is real, but sometime it is hard to recognize where the attacks are coming from. How do we know if we are fighting the world, the flesh, or the devil?

- The devil outwardly attacks with temptation to rebel against God. For instance, as you surf the web, an ad might invite you to a porn site, and you click on it. This is an attack from outside of yourself (you did not cause the temptation), but when you clicked on the temptation, you chose to violate God's word.
- The world distracts us from our walk with God, using care and concerns as well as pleasure and comforts. The devil loves to employ this worldly attack which keeps us running on a hamster wheel of distractions.
- Last, but not least, the battle is going on in our own hearts (flesh). "If only I had this, if only I didn't have these responsibilities…" Our longings and desires fight against our walk with God.

This war is also bigger than that.

THE BATTLE IN THE SPIRITUAL REALM. There is a reality that exists beyond what we can experience with our five senses. Scripture refers to this unseen realm when it talks about angels, demons, spiritual forces in heavenly places, and a real creature we call Satan. A battle is going on in the spiritual realms just as it is on earth:

Angels & Spiritual Beings		Satan & Demons
created to serve God and His people	VS	who desire to destroy God's people

The Bible gives us a picture of this battle in the story of Daniel. As a young Israelite, Daniel was taken as a captive to Babylon while his whole country was destroyed and ransacked. In spite of all the horrors he experienced, he held on tightly to God and was eventually awarded with a high position in Babylon's government. Throughout his life, Daniel continued to mourn for his people, and on one occasion, he spent three weeks fasting and praying for their future rescue. An angel finally arrived and explained to Daniel the astounding reason for the long-delayed response.

"Then he said to me, "Do not be afraid, Daniel, for from the first day that you set your heart on understanding this and on humbling yourself before your God, your words were heard, and I have come in response to your words. But the prince of the kingdom of Persia was standing in my way for twenty-one days; then behold, Michael, one of the chief princes, came to help me, for I had been left there with the kings of Persia." (Daniel 10:12-13, NASB)

Scripture gives us a clear picture here of a literal conflict in two realms. On earth, we see Daniel at war by the river: fasting and praying, pleading and insisting, persisting and agonizing. In the unseen realms, a pitched battle was raging between God's angels and evil spirits who didn't want to let God's message reach Daniel.

As He always does, God made the decision in heaven and worked on earth through the system He designed: believers' prayers bring His power to earth. Daniel interceded for his people as a prayer warrior, and God answered, but the angel messenger had to pass through a war zone to reach this persistent prayer warrior. Daniel's decisive battle to overcome evil was fought and won through his persistent prayer on earth. Prayer is the key to the Kingdom of God.

Even though we actually cannot see warfare taking place in the spiritual realm, the results are plainly visible to us. Look at the examples below and determine which way do you think the battle is going.

- Families praying together, whole congregations fasting together for a common cause, Christians sharing the Gospel message, a nurse compassionately caring for a patient, believers bring help and love to unwed mothers, a listening ear, food banks, community involvement, neighbors helping heighbors, and more of God's love for us being shown by us to others.

- Families devastated by divorce, men and women addicted to internet pornography, aborted or abandoned children,

> abusive relationships, IEDs or bombs ripping apart combatants and innocent bystanders, strained and damaged relationships, emotional instability, mental fatigue, physical exhaustion, unbridled anger, unforgiveness, pride, comparisons, insecurity, discord, fear, and so much more.

The war is on. Pray powerful prayers. Fight to win!

DON'T BE DISCOURAGED

Jesus tells his followers, "You will have many trials and sorrows on this battleground between good and evil, but I have already won the final battle. I'm preparing a special place for you in my eternal home (John 14:2). As you fight the good fight, remember how precious you are to me and that I have given you the power and legal authority to overcome evil in this world."

The devil builds roadblocks of doubt and firewalls of unbelief inside us to dampen the fires of our faith (Mark 9:19). He wants to stop us in our tracks even though God has given us everything we need to blow these barriers to smithereens. In Titus 2, we are encouraged to live in this evil world with wisdom, righteousness, and devotion to God, while we look forward with hope to that wonderful day when the glory of our great God and Savior, Jesus Christ, will be revealed.

No matter how hard we try, we can't will ourselves to believe. However, by God's grace we are in His Circle of Love, so we are armed with the chain reaction of praise, faith, prayer, overcoming evil, and reigning and ruling with Him. Alex Kendrick's film, "Facing the Giants," shows us an example of leaving doubt behind and reentering belief in the death crawl scene (available on Youtube.com).

> Shiloh Academy's football coach was facing tough circumstances in life, and his discouragement also infected the high school football team. After a long, agonizing night on his knees before God, Coach became convicted that he needed to praise God every day, no matter how bad his circumstances were. It changed him internally from wallowing powerlessly

in his own pitiful circumstances to an awe-filled recognition of God's presence in his life.

Coach tried to get his team to believe that they also had access to more strength than they could ever imagine. However, their unbelief and skepticism kept them from accepting this truth. A turning point came when the coach challenged Brock, a team leader, to do the "death crawl" for 20 yards.

Blindfolded, Brock crawled face down on hands and feet with a 160-pound teammate on his back. The team smirked and joked, but as Brock somehow passed the 20-, the 30-, the 40-, and finally the 50-yard line, the team's laughter and teasing remarks erupted into cheers and encouragement. Coach walked, then crawled next to Brock, encouraging him constantly: "Give your very best! Keep driving. Don't quit, Brock—don't quit until you have nothing left! I want everything you've got. I know it's hard, but you can do it. Keep going. You promised me your best. Give me more. Only 20 more steps."

Brock finally collapsed feeling defeated, until the coach said, "Look up Brock, you're in the end zone. You did it! You just carried a 160-pound man across the whole field in your arms."

Of course, this isn't a perfect picture of defeating unbelief, but it does show how much our faith affects warfare. Brock's coach encouraged him when he wanted to quit, reminded him to "keep going," to not sink back into unbelief. When we are at the end of our own strength, the Holy Spirit reminds us of the unimaginable power God provides. The devil whispers to us, "It would be so much easier to quit, to give up. All you have to do is step away from the battlefield. No one could blame you." The deceiver offers us the "easy way out," but the truth is, we need to overcome or be overcome.

So crash right through the roadblock of unbelief and remember: *Humble yourselves before God. Resist the devil, and he will flee from you. Come close to God, and God will come close to you* (James 4:7-8, NLT).

Back to the movie, as it ended, every issue in the coach's life was resolved. That isn't necessarily how God will answer our prayers, but His answers will always have the ultimate goal for each of us in mind—our salvation. When we focus on Him with praise, our faith is activated, God answers with power in response to our prayers, and all things are possible.

Explore and Exercise

1. In Romans 7:14-25, Paul expresses deep frustration with the reality that we have to fight the good fight on the home front, in our own hearts and minds. Even though we agree with God's law, we are often obedient to something else that lives in us—this is one of the most depressing and hopeless realities of our lives. Sin is evil, and the flesh is weak. We try to rationalize our sinful actions to make it appear that we have good reasons for our sin, but there really aren't any. Sin is an irrational act which has no easy, rational explanation.

   a. Paul admits his own wretched state as an unwilling slave to sin, a condition that brought him to the end of his own resources, totally unable to manage his own sin. As Christians, we struggle with the same truth. Explain why you believe it may or may not be important for us to recognize and agonize over our sinful condition as did Paul.

   b. Why does Paul, why do we, keep fighting this seemingly unwinnable war? What gives us hope? Answer in your own words or expand upon Paul's answer in verse 25.

2. Praising God daily, in any and all circumstances, is not a new tradition. For thousands of years, Jewish people have prayed "The Shema," every morning and evening as a way of expressing their devotion. It begins with praising God for who He is, a reminder that we are to love him as He loves us (Deuteronomy 6:4-5). The next verses tell God's people to leave reminders all around to help them think about God all the time (Deuteronomy 6: 6-8).

   a. Give some examples from the Bible of the kinds of things people did, built, wore, or said to remember the help that God had given them in the past?

   b. Today, most Christians don't add blue-corded tassels to their clothes or splash blood on the doorposts. Share some prompts you could incorporate as reminders of the love God has for you that fit your lifestyle. (For example, carry a rock in your pocket to symbolize "Jesus is my rock" or "He is not there; He is risen even as He said.")

3. We tend to think of our problems and struggles in non-spiritual, physical terms. Ephesians 6:12 tells us there is so much more to it—our biggest problems are spiritually rooted.

   a. Read 2 Kings 6:8-23 and Daniel 10:7-17. How do these Bible stories represent two different scenarios of activity that are taking place in the invisible realm around us?

   b. God allowed Daniel, Elisha, and Elisha's servant to bridge the gap to temporarily see into the spiritual realm.

      i. What advantages would be ours if, at our prayerful request, God granted us more spiritual vision? Does God still give similar visions to Christians today?

      ii. Describe the kind of protection and weapons God provides for us to overcome evil.

4. It is reported that ancient Chinese general and military strategist, Sun Tzu, taught: "Know thy enemy and know yourself; in a hundred battles, you will never be defeated. When you are ignorant of the enemy but know yourself, your chances of winning or losing are equal. If ignorant both of your enemy and of yourself, you are sure to be defeated in every battle."

   a. Make a list of the prominent roadblocks you usually experience as you pursue a close relationship with God.

   b. Who is the devil, and what designs does he have on you?

   c. Sun Tzu didn't mention the most important personage in this battle. Adapt the quote above to include God, an acknowledgement of the battle Christians are in, but one that ends with hope rather than defeat.

5. **Fight "The Good Fight" Challenge**. Reflect on a time when you thought you wouldn't make it or that you didn't have enough faith to endure a situation. Use the following ideas to help you be ready when the devil launches his next missile attack against you.

a. When your life gets turned upside down, how long does it take you to remember to pray? Think of a way to remind yourself that God is in control. For example, carry a matchbook to remind you to light the flame of faith, repeat the acronym **ASK** (**A**lways **S**eek the **K**ing), or follow an unhappy "Oh, no!" with the declaration "Oh, yes, He can!"

b. Choose a praise text or God-praise prompt that you could say in the middle of the chaos and say it out loud or in your mind. Write it down, carry it with you, memorize it, and practice it daily so that it will be readily available when you need it.

6. **Fight "The Good Fight" Challenge**. Read the Scripture passages below. Focus on how God equips you in the battle to overcome evil.

So humble yourselves before God. Resist the devil, and he will flee from you. Come close to God, and God will come close to you. Wash your hands, you sinners; purify your hearts, for your loyalty is divided between God and the world. Let there be tears for what you have done. Let there be sorrow and deep grief. Let there be sadness instead of laughter, and gloom instead of joy. Humble yourselves before the Lord, and he will lift you up in honor. (James 4:7-9, NLT)

Do not conform to the pattern of this world, but be transformed by the renewing of your mind. Then you will be able to test and approve what God's will is—his good, pleasing and perfect will. (Romans 12:2, NIV)

So remove your dark deeds like dirty clothes, and put on the shining armor of right living. Because we belong to the day, we must live decent lives for all to see. Don't participate in the darkness ... Instead, clothe yourself with the presence of the Lord Jesus Christ. And don't let yourself think about ways to indulge your evil desires. (Romans 13:12-14. NLT)

Form your battle plan and write it down. Using personal pronouns (I and me) or your name, explain to a classmate how the progression through praise—faith—prayer brings you God so that you can overcome evil. It might sound something like this:

"When life spirals out of control, I praise God and remember that He is bigger than all my problems, which fills me full of faith so that I trust that He always cares for me. I can talk with Him about everything—He listens and responds 24/7. When I don't have any more to give, God's infinite, powerful resources overcome all obstacles. I am part of a family—the family of God."

PART 4: CHAPTER 13

Onward Christian Soldiers

This is the battle plan God set up for us: we pray faithfully, and God supplies His power and authority.

We are all soldiers—each and every believer is in combat on the front lines in the fight to overcome evil. In 1869, William Sherwin published a hymn intended for use in Sunday Schools: "Sound the Battle Cry!"

SOUND the battle cry! See, the foe is nigh,
Raise the standard high for the Lord.
Gird your armour on; Stand firm every one;
Rest your cause upon His holy word.

Strong to meet the foe, Marching on we go,
While our cause we know must prevail.
Shield and banner bright, gleaming in the light,
Battling for the right, We ne'er can fail.

O thou God of all, hear us when we call,
Help us one and all by thy grace!
When the battle's done, and the victory won,
May we wear the crown before thy face.

Refrain:
Rouse, then, soldiers, rally round the banner!
Ready, steady, pass the word along;
Onward, forward, shout aloud hosanna!
Christ is captain of the mighty throng.

Some may think this is too militant, too inflammatory, or too scary for children, but remember that even the weakest and the youngest of believers have been given the weapons of praise, faith, and prayer that enable us to overcome evil. Yes, even our children are soldiers-in-training as believers, and sometimes they lead us.

The Bible makes it clear: We are in a battle we can't escape with an Enemy we can't see. When we confess Jesus as Lord and have the Spirit of God within us, Satan will launch everything he can to destroy our faith. That's why we're told to "stand firm" against his schemes (Ephesians 6:13).

> Christianity is like a nail. The harder you strike it, the deeper it goes.
> ~ Yaroslavsky, Chairman of Stalin's League of the Militant Godless in 1921

WE ARE SAVED AND SANCTIFIED SOLDIERS

Believers are "sanctified," set apart or "made holy," through Jesus Christ as we are vessels filled with the Holy Spirit of God (Hebrews 10:10 and 1 Peter 1:2). We have made a conscious, willing decision to dedicate our souls, minds, hearts, and bodies to God. Therefore, through the Holy Spirit, we are being renewed and our capacity to hold more of the fullness of God's love is expanding (Romans 12:1-2). (See: Appendix C: The Order of Salvation.)

What we, as individuals, truly believe about God affects what we believe about ourselves. The world might label us losers, not good enough, "one fry short of a happy meal," naughty, dumb, unlovable…egocentric, privileged, superior, or deserving. If we accept these labels as truth, how will we be able to trust that God loves us and chooses us to be His children and heirs?

Unless we can move "God is good to me" from simply head knowledge to trusting this truth in our hearts and souls, we will not be able to really believe that He loves us when hard things happen in our lives. This kind of faith is not something that we need to "strive" to do—it's God's grace-filled gift to us. God doesn't want you to try harder, but to trust Him more deeply. Stop trying. Praise Him to activate your faith and start trusting. Enter into relationship with Him through prayer. This will change everything in you.

May you experience the love of Christ, though it is too great to understand fully. Then you will be made complete with all the fullness of life and power that comes from God. (Ephesians 3:19, NLT)

God not only loves us; He provides for all the needs of His saved and sanctified soldiers (Ephesians 3:19) with both defensive gear and offensive weapons: Our armor consists of spiritual realities that believers can wear daily (Ephesians 6:10-18). We put on our soldierly habits by surrendering ourselves to the Lord and walking in close relationship with Him.

DEFENSE: THE ARMOR OF GOD. Ephesians 6 draws a picture of the armor that God has provided for us to wear to battle.

BELT OF TRUTH: *Stand your ground, putting on the belt of truth* (Ephesians 6:14, NLT). This belt is not a "what," but a "who"— Jesus surrounds you and holds you all together. **Whatever controls your mind, controls your identity,** so be dust-covered disciples walking closely with Christ. So when we really believe this is true and that the Holy Spirit dwells in us, it changes everything. For every child of God defeats evil in this world, and we achieve this victory through our faith (1 John 5:4, NLT).

Put on the BODY ARMOR OF GOD'S RIGHTEOUSNESS (Ephesians 6:14). When God looks at us, He sees Jesus' perfect record that replaces ours, but there's more. As apprentices in the faith, we are transforming and conforming our lives to Christ's righteousness through praise, activated faith, and continual prayer.

HELMET OF SALVATION. *Embrace the power of salvation's full deliverance, like a helmet to protect your thoughts from lies* (Ephesians 6:17, TPT). A helmet guards our heads, our brains, our center of thinking, so we continue to think: "I am saved, and God is faithful." God designed our brains to be malleable or changeable. That means that when we choose to think about our immense, almighty, faithful God, we wear a helmet that declares our salvation, and it is impenetrable (1 Corinthians 10:13).

SHIELD OF FAITH. *In every battle, take faith as your wrap-around shield, for it is able to extinguish the blazing arrows coming at you from the Evil One* (Ephesians 6:16, TPT). We know how to light the bonfire of our faith—by striking a match through praising God. Satan aims lies at our hearts, shooting fiery arrows as he tries to penetrate our shields. Head knowledge, logic, or our own efforts aren't strong enough to protect us. Instead, wrap yourself with faith by

repeating: "I am saved by grace through faith. I do not have to fear because I am adopted as a child and heir into the family of God. And if God is for me, who can be against me. Surely goodness and mercy will follow me all the days of my life, and I will dwell in the house of the Lord forever."

OFFENSE: THE AUTHORITY AND POWER THAT CHRIST HAS GIVEN US. *There is nothing flimsy about the weapons that every Christian wields. The weapons we fight with are not the weapons of the world. On the contrary, they have divine power to demolish strongholds* (2 Corinthians 10:4, NLT).

GOOD NEWS SHOES. *For shoes, put on the peace that comes from the Good News so that you will be fully prepared* (Ephesians 6:15, NLT). The Message version says it this way: *God's Word is an indispensable weapon.* It is your feet that carry you—your whole body—into the battle (Isaiah 52:7). Your body is a temple in which the Holy Spirit lives, and Satan cannot remain in the presence of Jesus. Step into the fight full of the Good News, and go on the offensive by sharing it in your thoughts, words, and actions. *The Word of God is a double-edged sword that cuts through the bone to the marrow* (Hebrews 4:12), and your ability to overcome evil is directly proportionate to your consistent presence with God, listening to His words. Read the Bible, memorize it, meditate, and pray in ongoing conversation. Saturate yourself in the fullness of God so that when life cuts you, you bleed God's words.

PRAY PERSISTENTLY. *Pray in the Spirit at all times and on every occasion. Stay alert and be persistent in your prayers for all believers everywhere* (Ephesians 6:18, NLT). Evangelist Phyllis Shirer compares a Christian who doesn't pray to someone who owns a refrigerator, but doesn't plug it into the power source; it just doesn't work. Praying powerful prayers is our divine power source. God gives us what we need to engage in battle in both the worldly and heavenly realms. When we boldly ask much of God for His Kingdom, we put the gospel into action and can declare Jesus' victory over Satan.

This is the battle plan God set up for us: we pray faithfully, and God supplies His power and authority.

WE WILL NOT BE SHAKEN

Has all this talk of soldiers and pitched battles frightened you? If so, you are not alone. Remember the first words of angelic messengers in the Bible: "Don't be afraid." If it was all up to us, we'd be in trouble, but God doesn't just thrown us into the water and say, "Sink or swim." He encourages us to jump in so that He can hold us up as He teaches us how to swim. More than that, we never swim alone.

> *The temptations in your life are no different from what others experience. And God is faithful. He will not allow the temptation to be more than you can stand. When you are tempted, he will show you a way out so that you can endure.* (1 Corinthians 10:13, NLT)

As saved and sanctified soldiers we are engaged in basic training—boot camp—to prepare for all elements of service: physical, mental, emotional, and spiritual. God provides the basic instruction and all the tools necessary to be on the front lines during the duration of our tour on earth.

Learning all the right stuff—head knowledge of God's word to us in the Bible—is an important part of our training as Christian soldiers, but boot camp doesn't stop there. Followers of Jesus are transformed as we learn to say what Jesus said, think the way Jesus thinks, and do what Jesus did, so that we can overcome evil with good (Romans 12:21). It's all possible because God has given us the same authority and power that He gave His Son Jesus Christ.

God designed each of us with the abilities and talents to complete the unique mission into which He has placed us. The Lord goes before each individual soldier and with all troops of the Church giving us the necessary weapons, strength, authority, and power. Through His death and resurrection, our victory has already been assured. We receive the same marching orders given to the disciples:

"It is not for you to know the times or dates the Father has set by his own authority. But you will receive power when the Holy Spirit comes on you; and you will be my witnesses in Jerusalem, and in all Judea and Samaria, and to the ends of the earth." (Acts 1:7-8, NIV)

"Be witnesses of God" is God's general commission for all of us, but fulfilling this mission will not look the same from one person to another. The Book of Acts gives us a few examples of this diversity:

- Paul was a zealous, hotheaded fanatic both before and after his conversion; someone who told it like it is. Paul left the life he knew to spread the Gospel throughout the world. It often put him in great danger, and his life on earth ended by execution. We'll meet Paul in heaven.

- Barnabas was "a good man, full of the Holy Spirit and faith, who was sent out as a missionary. This man, whose name means "Son of Encouragement," brought a great number of people to the Lord" (Acts 11:24). He traveled with Paul, and then with Mark to Cypress spreading the Good News. We'll meet Barnabas in heaven.

- Timothy was a young man of mixed heritage: his father was Greek while his mother and grandmother were Jews who converted to Christianity. His exceptional reputation among local Christians (Acts 16) and familiarity with both the Jewish and Greco-Roman cultures made him an excellent protégé for Paul. This enthusiastic, faith-filled youngster volunteered for exposure on the front lines of the spiritual battle field at an early age and fought the good fight throughout the rest of his life. We'll meet Timothy in heaven.

- Priscilla was a woman of Jewish heritage and one of the earliest known Christian converts who lived in Rome (Romans 16). Her home was a safe haven for followers of The Way. She is often thought to have been the first example of a female preacher or teacher in early church history. We'll meet Priscilla in heaven.

- Lydia lived and worked in Philippi, dealing in textiles colored with the purple dye for which the region was famous (Acts 16). Her wealth allowed her to live independently in a spacious house. A Gentile by birth and a religious seeker, this successful businesswoman opened her heart, her home, and her life to following God, providing a home base for Paul and area converts. We'll meet Lydia in heaven.

- An unnamed Philippian jailer was just trying to do his job when an unusual earthquake opened all the cell doors of the prisoners. Facing inevitable execution from his Roman superiors, the jailer determined to kill himself. When Paul and Silas called out to assure him that no one had escaped, the jailer fell on his face at their feet and asked, "What shall I do to be saved?" "Believe in God," they answered. In that moment, he became a new man in Christ, and his life was transformed. His first act was to wash and tend the wounds of the prisoners who had repaid his cruel treatment by telling him God's great plan of salvation. The Bible doesn't tell us more about his life except that "he was a changed man." We'll meet this jailer in heaven.

- The brothers and sisters in Christ who met in Lydia's house knew how to wield prayer as a weapon in the battle against evil. They were just ordinary, everyday people who prayed powerful prayers together for the protection and release of Paul and Silas. God answered their prayers with a miraculous earthquake. As a result, Paul and Silas were eventually released by the frightened magistrates. We'll meet the Philippian believers in heaven.

Were all of these people in full-time ministry? No, but they all worked for God wherever they were and in whatever they did. This is our destiny, our calling, as Christian Soldiers. Will we ask God, "Who am I that you should ask me to do this?" like Moses did when God revealed that he was the one who would lead the Israelite slaves out of Egypt? The answer we hear is the same as the one Moses received, "You're with Me." That's the important thing—we are with God and in God, a part of His family. Whatever we do, He has us covered.

We are at war, so we fight to overcome or be overcome. Our mission in God's army is as real as that of the Biblical warriors listed above. We need to constantly be ready to answer the call. Satan's fiery arrows can cause great harm when we are carelessly half-dressed in God's armor. Be prepared. When the Holy Spirit knocks on the doors of our hearts, we have to welcome Him into every room. He provides a chain reaction that will bring us to battle-ready status at any time.Strike the match with praise. It only takes a spark to ignite faith and trust in God so it blazes like a bonfire in our hearts. No matter what is happening or how deeply we have sunk into disaster, we are never out of range of God's communication system. We pray; He responds.

So, here we are, all dressed for the occasion in Ephesians 6 armor, on whatever battlefield against evil that God has placed us. And He tells us, "Do not be afraid!"

> *Because you are close to me and always available,*
> *my confidence will never be shaken,*
> *for I experience your wrap-around presence every moment.*
> *My heart and soul explode with joy—full of glory!*
> (Psalm 16:8-9, TPT)

Explore and Exercise

1. Charles Haddon Spurgeon, a noted British preacher in the 1800s, said, "You must either be overcome by evil, or you must yourself overcome evil: one of the two. You cannot let evil alone, and evil will not let you alone. You must fight, and in the battle you must either conquer or be conquered."

    a. Draw a picture (or write a description) of yourself as a "fighter of evil" or an "overcomer." How do you prepare yourself for battle?

    b. What is your primary battleground: home, work, social media, friendships, all of the above, other? What weapons have you put to the most use in the last week?

2. Compare and contrast the two quotes below:

    "The dictionary is the only place where success comes before work!" ~ Mark Twain

    What good is it, dear brothers and sisters, if you say you have faith but don't show it by your actions? Can that kind of faith save anyone? Suppose you see a brother or sister who has no food or clothing, and you say, "Good-bye and have a good day; stay warm and eat well"—but then you don't give that person any food or clothing. What good does that do? So you see, faith by itself isn't enough. Unless it produces good deeds, it is dead and useless. (James 2:14-17, NLT)

    a. Explain the meaning of Mark Twain's quote. Does it hold true when applied to Christianity? If we equate "success" with "salvation," in what way does Twain's work ethic clash with God's salvation?

    b. On the surface, it might appear that James is arguing against "we are saved by grace, not works" (Ephesians 2:8). What point do you think James is trying to make?

    c. Compare Romans 12 to James 2:14-17. How do these Scriptures speak into our mission to overcome evil with good?

Chapter 13: Onward Christian Soldiers

3. In a 2019 women's volleyball competition, teams from many countries vied for the opportunity to compete in the 2020 Olympics. The team from Bulgaria, who hadn't been to the Olympics since 1980, was not considered a strong contender, so it was a big surprise when they beat the highly-seeded U.S. team in the first set (best out of five). The U.S. team won the second, but Bulgaria managed to eke out the win in set 3. Set 4 was a real nail-biter until the U.S. team surged at the end for a big win. The teams continually traded the lead during the last set.

   The commentators pointed out that the U.S. team had an advantage because they had played in extremely tough competitions for years and had experienced wins after near-defeats against great odds. The sportscasters speculated that the U.S. players' belief that they could win, gained through experience, was a deciding factor that helped them to overcome the Bulgarian team.

   a. Discuss the idea: "what you believe affects the outcome of an athletic competition." Do you agree? Describe how your experiences might influence your beliefs?

   b. What chance do new believers have to defeat evil without experience or recognition of God's previous work in their lives? What is the role of a more experienced athlete in a team effort? How might we apply this to Christians and the Church?

   c. What does it take for an athlete or athletic team to qualify for the Olympics? Compare this kind of effort to Christian soldiers "marching as to war."

4. Read the verses below.

   So now there is no condemnation for those who belong to Christ Jesus. And because you belong to him, the power of the life-giving Spirit has freed you from the power of sin that leads to death. (Romans 8:1-2, NLT)

And they have defeated him [the devil] by the blood of the Lamb and by their testimony. And they did not love their lives so much that they were afraid to die. (Revelation 12:11, NLT)

a. The Bible teaches that evil did not overcome Jesus—He was victorious over sin and death. How would you explain that idea to a 6-year-old when he asks, "If I'm free, how come I still do naughty things? Does that mean I'm going to die if I'm naughty?"

b. Revelation 12:11 implies that we may be called to martyrdom, but not to be afraid, because we are assured of our future—our future is victorious. A person who does not believe in God might ask, "So what good is that? If you're dead, how could you call that overcoming evil? It seems like evil won." How would you answer these questions?

5. **Overcomers' Challenge:** Read the verses below.

[God spoke through Ezekiel] "I looked for someone to stand up for me against all this, to repair the defenses of the city, to take a stand for me and stand in the gap to protect this land so I wouldn't have to destroy it. I couldn't find anyone. Not one. So I'll empty out my wrath on them, burn them to a crisp with my hot anger, serve them with the consequences of all they've done. Decree of God, the Master." (Ezekiel 22:30, MSG)

"If I ever shut off the supply of rain from the skies or order the locusts to eat the crops or send a plague on my people, and my people, my God-defined people, respond by humbling themselves, praying, seeking my presence, and turning their backs on their wicked lives, I'll be there ready for you: I'll listen from heaven, forgive their sins, and restore their land to health. From now on I'm alert day and night to the prayers offered at this place." (2 Chronicles 7:13-14, MSG)

My purpose in writing is simply this: that you who believe in God's Son will know beyond the shadow of a doubt that you have eternal life, the reality and not the illusion. And how bold and free we then become in his presence, freely asking according to his will, sure that he's listening. And if we're confident that he's listening, we know that what we've asked for is as good as ours. (John 4:13-15, MSG)

a. What part does prayer play in overcoming evil?

b. If God doesn't need our prayers, why does He wait for us to pray to release His power?

c. Ask God to speak to your heart about what He wants you to pray about. Ask Him to show you and wait quietly for His answer. Commit to a period of persistent prayer for whatever God has laid on your heart.

PART 5
Reign and Rule with Christ

*May your Kingdom come soon.
May your will be done on earth
as it is in heaven.* (Matthew 6:10, NLT)

The reason we exercise this chain reaction daily is to maintain a devoted fellowship between God and his people, a union that reflects the Garden of Eden in our sin-tained world. As we walk in close relationship with God, we realize our position as grace-equipped people who rule and reign with Christ on earth (NOW) and will do so for all eternity (NOT YET).

The creation mandate came from the heart of God when He said:

> *Let us make man in our image, in our likeness, and let them rule over the fish of the sea and the birds of the air, over the livestock, over all the earth, and over the creatures that move along the ground." So, God created man in his own image, in the image of God he created him; male and female he created them.* (Genesis 1:26-27, NIV)

The Psalmist celebrated this reality in praise to God:

> *You made him (humankind) ruler over the works of your hands; you put everything under his feet…O Lord, our Lord, how majestic is your name in all the earth!* (Psalm 8:6 & 9, NIV)

And Revelation tells us about the final defeat of Satan and death:

> *… For the Lord God will give them light. And they will reign forever and ever.* (Revelation 22:5, NIV)

What God wants to give us is always far better than what we want Him to give us. God's promise to provide frees us to concern ourselves only with obedience to Him. We should never settle for second best because we only see today. God sees the implications for eternity.
~ Wayne Stiles, 8-/26/19 blog on www.waynestiles.com

PART 5: CHAPTER 14
Story Time, Past and Present

Let your roots grow down into him, and let your lives be built on him. Then your faith will grow strong in the truth you were taught... (Colossians 2:7, NLT)

LIVING IN THE KINGDOM OF GOD ON EARTH

Biblical Vignettes of Bearing Holy Spirit Fruit

The fundamental fact of existence is that this trust in God, this faith, is the firm foundation under everything that makes life worth living. It's our handle on what we can't see. The act of faith is what distinguished our ancestors, set them above the crowd. (Hebrews 11:1-2, MSG)

LOVING, FAITHFUL RUTH (RUTH 1:6-18)

Excerpt from Less Than a Widow *by Kathleen Evenhouse*

As Ruth attaches water skins to their donkey's pack, Naomi talks quietly to Orpah.

"...stay here with your family."

"I can't...I love you." Orpah chokes the words out through tears.

"And I love you. That's why I want you to stay in Moab."

"But Killion..."

Naomi almost shouts as she interrupts Orpah. "Is dead! Killion is dead. Both my sons and my husband are dead. We are nothing—widows without power or protection—how can I love you and want that kind of a life for you?"

Naomi calms herself with a deep breath and touches Orpah's cheeks with her worn hand. "Look at me. I'm too old for any man to want me. I won't bear another son, and even if I did, you'd be too old for childbearing by the time he grew up. I have nothing to give you."

"But it wouldn't be right to leave you."

"Orpah, dear darling Orpah, you have a future here in Moab—your family is here. There is nothing for you in Bethlehem. Yahweh has emptied my life of all that is good. Stay here, marry again, have babies, be happy. Do this for me, because I love you."

Orpah looks back toward the city gates where her mother and sisters are still waving good-bye. The war inside between loyalty to Naomi and common sense are tearing her apart.

Ruth put her arms around Orpah and whispers in her ear, "Don't worry about Naomi. I'll look after her."

"No, Ruth! What's true for Orpah is true for you, too." Naomi's voice is hard and angry again.

"I'm sorry, Mother, but it's not. Orpah's home is here with her family, her people, and her gods. My heart left Moab and her gods a long time ago, and now my body will follow it. Your people are my people; your God is my God. I swear in Yahweh's name that where you die, I will die, and that's where I will be buried."

Naomi points to the crying women at the city gates. "Your mother and sisters are waiting for you, Orpah, my child."

Orpah takes a bag of figs from her shoulder and gives it to Ruth, kisses her on both cheeks, then kisses Naomi. Her first few steps toward her family are tentative, but soon she's running, and they move to surround her.

Naomi grabs Ruth's arm—hard. "Ruth…"

"I am just as stubborn as Naomi," Ruth thinks. Drawing her thumb across her throat as if cutting it with a knife, she tells her mother-in-law firmly, "May Yahweh do this to me if I break my vow."

WAITING FOR THE MESSIAH (LUKE 2:25-38)

Anna and Simeon: Prayers Fulfilled

Luke introduced Anna as a prophetess—a woman who was uniquely devoted to declaring the word of God. Everything we know about her we learn in three short verses. She was a faithful servant of God, exhibited steadfast devotion to the Lord, and was constantly involved in a ministry of prayer and fasting. She had been married for seven years, but that was a lifetime ago as she had been a widow for 84 years. This elderly woman could always be found on the temple grounds. Perhaps she had a modest chamber in the outer courts, as did the priests who traveled to Jerusalem to do their two-week annual service. Perhaps she had been a caretaker in the temple, but by now she was too old for any such work.

Those who knew Anna considered her to be a most extraordinary woman. She was consumed with prayer, and so eager to receive God's blessing that she simply took no interested in eating—she fasted to focus on God. What did Anna pray about? We aren't told specifics, but surely one of her main subjects was an earnest plea for the coming of the Messiah, which was a prayer of all faithful believers in Israel at that time.

Luke also tells us about Simeon, a good man who lived in the prayerful expectancy of help for Israel. The Holy Spirit had revealed to Simeon that he would see the Messiah before he died and led him to the temple steps as Joseph and Mary arrived with baby Jesus. He gathered the tiny one in his arms and declared a blessing.

> *"... With my own eyes I've seen your salvation; it's now out in the open for everyone to see: A God-revealing light to the non-Jewish nations, and of glory for your people Israel. (Luke 2:30-32)*

Simeon then gave Mary a glimmer of what was to come: *failure and recovery, pain and rejection, and many brought to new faith.* And Anna was there to witness this interchange, which brought an anthem of praise pouring from her lips.

"He's here!" she cried out to everyone she met. "The Messiah has come—the one who we have been waiting for. I saw him today, right here in the temple."

Anna's life was simple, but not simplistic. She lived in God's truth.

LOVING KINDNESS (LUKE 10:3-36)

Jesus Responds to the Question, "Who Is My Neighbor?"

A Jewish man was traveling from Jerusalem to Jericho, and on the way he was attacked by robbers. They stripped him of his clothes, beat him up, and disappeared, leaving him at death's door. Soon after, a priest came upon the scene, but he moved to the side to avoid the blood contamination and continued on his way. Another man, a Levite temple assistant, showed up. He heard the injured man's groans, but also hurried past.

The next traveler walking this road was a Samaritan, a despised outsider. He heard the man's moans, and his heart went out to him. He pulled his pack from his donkey and tore a shift into strips. After cleaning the wounds, he wrapped them with his former shift, and gave the man a drink of wine. With great effort, he helped the wounded man onto his donkey, and led him down the road to an inn. There he made him as comfortable as possible and cared for him throughout the night.

The next morning he gave the innkeeper two silver coins. "'Take good care of him. If it costs any more, put it on my bill—I'll pay you on my way back."

CHANGE YOUR LIFE (ACTS 2:36-47)

Peter's Sermon on Pentecost
Excerpt from The Message, by Eugene Peterson

"All Israel, then, know this: There's no longer room for doubt—God made him Master and Messiah, this Jesus whom you killed on a cross."

[37] Cut to the quick, those who were there listening asked Peter and the other apostles, "Brothers! Brothers! So now what do we do?"

38-39 Peter said, "Change your life. Turn to God and be baptized, each of you, in the name of Jesus Christ, so your sins are forgiven. Receive the gift of the Holy Spirit. The promise is targeted to you and your children, but also to all who are far away—whomever, in fact, our Master God invites."

40 He went on in this vein for a long time, urging them over and over, "Get out while you can; get out of this sick and stupid culture!"

41-42 That day about three thousand took him at his word, were baptized and were signed up. They committed themselves to the teaching of the apostles, the life together, the common meal, and the prayers.

43-45 Everyone around was in awe—all those wonders and signs done through the apostles! And all the believers lived in a wonderful harmony, holding everything in common. They sold whatever they owned and pooled their resources so that each person's need was met.

46-47 They followed a daily discipline of worship in the Temple followed by meals at home, every meal a celebration, exuberant and joyful, as they praised God. People in general liked what they saw. Every day their number grew as God added those who were saved.

MIRACLE OF LIFE (ACTS 9:36-42)

Dorcas Is Returned to Life

They had done all they could: washed her body, combed and dressed her hair, and covered her with a linen cloth. But the widows couldn't bear to leave the house in which the body of their beloved benefactor lay. Her name was Tabitha (which in Greek is Dorcas).

"Dorcas didn't talk much. I think she was a shy person at heart."

"She was a good listener, though; she never forgot anything I told her."

"I think Dorcas said everything she needed to say with her needle and thread."

"Yes, and with food. I never left her house without a gift of bread or figs."

"I helped wash her body, but I still can't believe she's really dead! What will we do without her?"

Peter stood in the entry to the upstairs room with the two men who had fetched him from Lydda. He watched as the women alternately wailed with sorrow and comforted each other. Dorcas had not only been their benefactor, she had been their dear friend.

"Who is that?" One woman nodded toward the men stepping onto the rooftop.

"Where? Oh, look! The apostle Peter has come!"

The women pulled him to the doorway, all taking at once: "Look at this coat Dorcas made for me!" "We had nothing, and sister Dorcas never let us go hungry." "I wanted to pay, so she asked me fetch water in exchange for this robe." "Just a few days ago she was laughing with us, and now she's gone." "She was always so kind, I can't believe she's dead." And the wailing began again.

Peter held up his hand for silence. "Please leave me alone with your beloved friend." Reluctantly, with backward glances and stifled sobs, the women slowly left the room. One positioned herself so that she could see into the room without being seen.

Peter knelt and prayed. The observer mimed praying to the others. The women waited anxiously, and some knelt and mouthed silent prayers. And they waited. And waited. "Ssst," the watcher got their attention and mimed walking with two fingers, stopping beside the bed. The women held their breath and strained their ears.

"Tabitha, get up."

Some shook their heads at the absurdity of Peter's words. Some gasped, and other shushed them, straining to listen for a response. Some raised their eyes and hands to heaven in supplication.

Chapter 14: Story Time, Past and Present

The bed creaked, and the observer clapped her hand to her mouth, tears flowing down her cheeks. "What?!" hissed the others. "Tell us!" She pointed to the doorway, and there stood Dorcas, leaning on Peter's arm.

"The Lord has returned her to you," Peter told them.

This good news became known all over Joppa, and many put their trust in the Lord.

AT HOME IN THE THRONE ROOM OF GOD

A Modern-Day Story of Praise and Prayer

Weeks after the funeral, Randy and I got together in a coffee shop and told "Kathy stories:" how they met, how she drew him to Christ, and the ups and downs of life. He told me about their tough times and how they were followed by periods of growing faith. The stories gradually became filled with signs and wonders—miracles of physical and spiritual healing—a sign of God's Kingdom of God here on earth.

Kathy's life is an example for us of the progression of praise: As we praise God in all circumstances, our faith is activated and it grows, enabling us to pray powerful prayers to overcome evil, so that we may reign and rule with Christ in this world and in eternity to come.

~ ~ ~

At first, the only thing that made this weekend remarkable was changing the clocks to Daylight Savings Time. Routine blood tests on Friday had told Kathy that she was still in control of her sixteen-year fight with diabetes, and on a Saturday drive, Randy and Kathy laughed about the joys and pains of growing old together.

Saturday night was a special time: a Solomon's Porch gathering with others to worship and soak in the presence of a Holy God. Their friend and fellow worshiper, Linda, tells us, "As we worshipped, Randy sat in a chair with Kathy on the floor in front of him, her head resting on his lap. The two of them, fully surrendered to God and to each other, resting in His presence together, painted a picture of a Holy Moment that I will always treasure."

Sunday began early. Randy and Kathy prayed for blessings and God's strong presence throughout their church building. Active prayer warriors, the couple then met in the Prayer Room with a number of people seeking God's help and guidance. Later, a young woman they had prayed with earlier in the morning returned requesting that Kathy and Randy join her in meeting meet with church elders, so they did. They then invited this young woman to join them for lunch at a local restaurant, where they talked into the afternoon. Heading home for a quick nap. The couple returned to church for a monthly evening service focused on praise and prayer.

Home once more, bedtime was delayed by a family phone call, and it wasn't until 11:30 p.m. that Kathy finally turned out the lights. At 2 a.m., Randy turned them back on to investigate what it was that had woken him up.

He discovered that Kathy's life on earth had ended; just like that. Without warning, Kathy transitioned from life on earth to eternity.

At the funeral, the pastor smiled broadly and said, "Kathy is now present in the throne room of God. It is a room she knows very well because she spent so much of her earthly life in that very room in deep conversation with God."

Months later, Randy found a letter addressed to him hidden among Kathy's journals. Written more than ten years earlier, Kathy listed the scriptures that made up the foundation of her faith-filled life. She also listed songs and requests for individuals to act as readers at her funeral. She had addressed the envelope to Randy, but never mailed or delivered it. The requested Scripture passages were the foundation for Kathy in both her life and her death:

(Lamentations 3:22-24) *God's compassions never fail; they are new every morning.*

(Deuteronomy 7:9) *Know that the Lord your God the faithful God and keeps His covenant of love.*

(Psalm 27; 1 & 14) *The Lord is my light and my salvation—whom shall I fear?*

(Psalm 103) *Praise the Lord, my soul.*

(Isaiah 40:29-31) *We will soar on wings like eagles; run and not grow weary, walk and not be faint.*

(Matthew 11:28-30) *Come to me, all you who are weary and burdened, and I will give you rest.*

(Romans 6:23) *For the wages of sin is death, but the gift of God is eternal life in Christ Jesus our Lord.*

(Colossians 2:6-7) *Continue to live your lives in him, rooted and built up in him, strengthened in the faith as you were taught, and overflowing with thankfulness.*

(James 1:5) *If any of you lacks wisdom, you should ask God, who gives generously to all without finding fault, and it will be given to you.*

(John 3:16-18) *For God so loved the world that he gave his one and only Son, that whoever believes in him shall not perish but have eternal life.*

Explore and Exercise

1. Hebrews 11 tells us about people whose lives demonstrated a firm faith in the promises of God even though they may not have yet received the fulfillment of those promises. Not only did they bear witness to God, He bore witness to them, affirming their lives of faith.

    Each one of these people of faith died not yet having in hand what was promised, but still believing. How did they do it? They saw it way off in the distance, waved their greeting, and accepted the fact that they were transients in this world. People who live this way make it plain that they are looking for their true home. If they were homesick for the old country, they could have gone back any time they wanted. But they were after a far better country than that—heaven country. You can see why God is so proud of them, and has a City waiting for them. (Hebrews 11:13-16, MSG)

    a. "This world is not my home, I'm just a-passing through; my treasures are laid up somewhere beyond the blue." Share how the words of this old hymn can be seen in the lives of the people in our Biblical stories or the people of faith described in Hebrews 11?

    b. The chorus to this hymn: "O Lord, You know I have no friend like You, if heaven's not my home, then, Lord, what will I do? The angels beckon me from heaven's open door, and I can't feel at home in this world anymore." Give a concrete example of one way this kind of attitude might be visible in your life.

    c. Have you prayed for release from a tough situation or condition in your life (as did Paul and Jesus), without receiving the specific answer that you prayed for? [Paul prayed for release from a physical condition (2 Corinthians 2:1-10), and Jesus asked if there was any way to fulfill His mission without the terrible death He would have to endure (Matthew 26:39).] How has that affected your faith?

2. Read Jesus' parable of the ten bridesmaids in Matthew 25:1-13. Those listening to Jesus would be familiar with this scenario: a bride and her bridesmaids, lamps lit and burning, waited at the bride's home for the bridegroom to arrive, usually after dark. When he arrived, they would hold up their lamps to illuminate a dancing parade of celebration leading to where the final event—the wedding—would take place.

> HISTORICAL NOTE. In Semitic societies, the first part of the marriage took place when the families met together to discuss details of the bride's trousseau and her bride price. Then the groom's family had to fulfill their part of the contract: a private room added to the house; supplies such as grain, cooking oil, and spices; garments for the wedding party; and jewels for the bride—to be delivered to the bride's father before the wedding could take place. Accumulating these things could take months or years.
>
> The lamps the bridal party tended were small, about the size of a hand. These shallow, covered clay dishes had two holes: one to add oil and one to hold a wick. If the wick burned down too low, it would smoke and eventually go out, so close attention to the wick and the supply of oil was important.

After telling the parable, Jesus summed up its meaning clearly: You also must be ready all the time, for the Son of Man will come when least expected (Luke 12:40).

   a. How does this parable speak into the story of Kathy, whose sudden death was unexpected? Where would Kathy have fit into the story?

   b. Compare these bridesmaids to the seeds in Jesus' parable of the Sower and the explanation he gave to his disciples (Luke 8:5-15). Identify the two groups of bridesmaids by what kinds of seeds they might represent.

   c. Read Jesus' explanation of the parable of the bridesmaids to His disciples (Matthew 25:14) one more time. Compare the father of the groom to our heavenly Father who is making preparations for the End Times—for the wedding of His Son with His Church.

    i. Read Romans 9:22-23. Why might the groom, who will provide garments for the entire wedding party, be delaying his arrival?

    ii. Write out the following verses: Psalm 119:105, 2 Samuel 22:29, Proverbs 6:23. According to this image, what do the bridesmaids' lamps represent to us, God's Church, today?

    1. What is the purpose of the lamps in the parable? What does this tell us to do with "our lamps" today to be ready when the groom comes?

    2. Explain why a wick is a key part of every lamp? What does the wick represent in our lives, in our churches?

    iii. Read 1 Samuel 16:13 and Acts 10:38.

    What does oil represent in the Bible? What does the oil represent to us today? In our parable, what was the distinguishing characteristic of the bridesmaids who were ready and those who were not?

    iv. Read John 14:26. Explain the part that the oil—the Holy Spirit—plays as we read the Word of God?

    v. What do these verses and this parable tell us about embracing both the Word of God and the Holy Spirit and His gifting in our churches: in our worship, in our activities, and in our fellowship?

3. The purpose statement of Third Church in Pella, Iowa reads:

Why we exist: People who come in contact with the Third Church body will experience the Fruit of the Spirit, an ever-deepening intimacy with the Triune God and an ever-increasing sacrificial generosity of the Body.

What we do: Sending servant-hearted disciples with a passion for Jesus into the world.

Chapter 14: Story Time, Past and Present 199

Where we are going: Cultivating Kingdom People who flourish in exile—bringing light and hope in a post-Christian context.

   a. Choose one of the biblical short stories in this chapter and explain how you saw the Kingdom of God in their words and actions. In other words, how did they demonstrate love for God and others; make God known; share their time, talents, or treasures; overcome evil, or create disciples?

   b. Share a similar experience in which you had an opportunity to reflect God: by making a hard choice; giving up time, energy, and resources; living in harmonious relationship with others; sharing what you have despite dangers or cost; or relying on Holy Spirit enabling to overcome evil.

4. **Reign and Rule Challenge.** Do you know the central motivating aims of your life? Your life purpose can guide decisions, influence behavior, shape goals, offer a sense of direction and create meaning. What part does God play in your purpose statement?

   a. Do some research to read and understand the purpose statement of your church, your place of employment, or your school. Think about whether or not this purpose is being fulfilled, and list some ways that you are involved in fulfilling that purpose.

   b. Talk with your family. Do you have a unified belief or goal? How does that play out in your interactions with each other, with friends, and in your community?

   c. Ask God about the purpose for your life. Listen for His reply. Write a purpose statement for yourself

PART 5: CHAPTER 15

You Just Thank the Lord

Who is standing against Satan's rule in human affairs? We are, you and me, both as individuals and corporately as The Church.

PEOPLE GET READY

In 1965, The Impressions released a gospel-inspired song written by Curtis Mayfield called "People Get Ready." He used images from his church upbringing, such as: get on board the train to Jordan, faith, hope, and no need for a ticket—just get on board.

Christians, we're on board that train—we hopped on board when we accepted Jesus as our Lord and Savior. Our destination is to reign and rule with Christ, which has always been God's intention for humankind and is also our current reality. Our poor choices and the resulting sin would have made that impossible if not for the "Jesus train." When we get on board, we leave the baggage of our sin in Jesus' hands, and we are renewed and transformed as the journey progresses.

We're on board the Jesus train, and we have an official passport—the Holy Spirit who lives in each one of us who believe in Jesus Christ as our Lord and Savior (Ephesians 1:13-14).

Jesus' disciples, the women who followed Him, His mother Mary, and His brothers were the first ones to receive this "passport." At the time, they were hiding in an upper room in Jerusalem, as frightened and as confused as they had been when Jesus was crucified, but they were obediently waiting without knowing what was coming (Luke 24:46-49). "Jesus left us alone again. What are we going to do?" "Wait here as He told us to do." "But what are we waiting for?" "I don't know, but let's pray" (Acts 1:13-14).

The disciples obeyed in spite of their fear of being killed as their rabbi had been. Of course, they all had heard Jesus say, "stay in the city until you have been clothed with power from on high," but the meaning of His words hadn't penetrated into their being. Jesus had also told them to do the impossible, *"go and make disciples of all the nations"* (Matthew 28:18-21).

Fear and confusion were roadblocks that blocked Jesus' followers from their connection, their attachment, and their faith in Jesus Christ. Until, **as they prayed, they experienced Pentecost.**

When the Feast of Pentecost came, they were all together in one place. Without warning there was a sound like a strong wind, gale force—no one could tell where it came from. It filled the whole building. Then, like a wildfire, the Holy Spirit spread through their ranks, and they started speaking in a number of different languages as the Spirit prompted them. (Acts 2:1-4, MSG)

At the sound of a rushing wind and tongues of flames—when the Holy Spirit entered into each one of them—they thought, believed, said, and did things beyond their own abilities. **They could follow God's calling for their lives because they received the presence and power of God.**

Jesus' followers were imperfect people, as we are, in the process of transforming. God asked them and is asking us to do the impossible—to strive at something we can never achieve—which is the perfect definition of frustration!

But is frustration what God intends for us? NO! **For we have also experienced Pentecost. He's given us the Holy Spirit who dwells in each one of us.**

The Kingdom of God on earth is a paradox. The Oxford dictionary defines a paradox as "a seemingly absurd or self-contradictory statement or proposition that when investigated or explained may prove to be well founded or true." Faith challenges abound: How can the Kingdom of God exist in this war-torn, sin-filled, me-focused world?

The paradox of the Kingdom of God is that it is here, hiding in plain sight, but many can't see it (Acts 28:26-28). And those of us who are believers may be content to sit in the train station instead of hopping on board. We've been vaccinated with enough of Jesus Christ that we don't get a fever—we're not on fire for Him—so we stay comfortably in the station. Are our hearts calloused and blocked so we can't see what is hidden right in front of our eyes?

To move forward in the fire of faith, we need to get aboard the "Jesus train." We have both the Word and the Spirit, the salvation ticket and the passport. We don't depend on our imperfect selves, instead our power, calling, and love come from God. The Holy Spirit is our passport, our fuel, and our strength; He will remain in us and for us until our full redemption at the resurrection for God's praise and glory.

Know this truth! God has a calling for every believer! In fact, you are a solution to something in this world, to some situation, to some people group. Whoever, wherever, whatever that looks like, **God has called you to reign and rule with Christ, bringing His Kingdom to earth and for eternity.**

THE KINGDOM OF GOD: NOW AND NOT YET

When Jesus taught us to pray in Luke 11, the prayer included: *Your kingdom come, your will be done, on earth as it is in heaven.* How does God's Kingdom exist on this sin-filled earth?

Author and missionary, Arthur Glasser, traced the Kingdom of God throughout Scripture and describes it in two ways: (1) a realm we presently enter (NOW), and (2) a realm we will enter in the future (NOT YET).

> *Dear friends, NOW we are children of God, and what we will be has NOT YET been made known. But we know that when Christ appears, we shall be like him, for we shall see him as he is.* (1 John 3:2, NIV)

We are children of the King now, united with Him as temples in which the Holy Spirit dwells. We are saved by grace, God's masterpieces, created anew and in the process of transforming to be more and more like Him (Ephesians 2:6-10). And while we are experiencing God's Kingdom here on earth, we know—because God has promised—that there is more to come in the future ages.

Our NOW is just a reflection of the future physical reality—our NOT YET—that will come into being when Jesus Christ returns to earth. Someday, at God's chosen time, both Kingdoms will be in sync (1 Corinthians 13:12).

The Kingdom of God on earth **IS NOT**:

- **NOT** the belief that Christ's Kingdom is in full operation here and now.
- **NOT** the belief that prayer can claim earthly prosperity or fulfill our own desires.
- **NOT** the belief that people need never be sick or poor because the riches of the kingdom are available to them right now.
- Just as prayer is not a vending machine in which we make a choice and manipulate God to give us what we desire, the Kingdom purpose is **NOT** to bring us comfort in this world.

The Kingdom of God on earth **IS**:

- **IS** Pentecost—the Holy Spirit lives in us and we listen to His voice (1 John 2:27; Galatians 5:16-17).
- **IS** the Church. As believers, we represent God as one body, and each one of us individually is a part of that body (1 Corinthians 12:27).
- **IS** living a holy life (1 Timothy 1:9-11; Matthew 25:34-36) in order to reflect His light, so that others can see and glorify our Father in Heaven (Matthew 5:14-16).
- **IS** *not of this world* (John 18:36), but instead infiltrates this world as yeast spreads through dough or a tree bears fruit.
- **IS** total dependence on God. Remember that God tells us to receive Him as though we were a child (Mark 10:15), to spend time with Him so that we "know the mind of Christ" (1 Corinthians 2:12).

The Kingdom of God NOW is all about our present ride on the "Jesus train," going on a journey to the promised, NOT YET fully revealed Kingdom of God. During the journey, we continually loop from praise to growing faith so that we can pray powerful prayers to overcome evil and reign and rule with Christ on earth and forever. It is on this circular track that we see God's Kingdom reflected on earth—we are reigning and ruling with Christ in His Kingdom on earth NOW. And we are looking into the future, into the eternal promise, when we will be able to eliminate step four in the chain reaction—overcoming evil—because God's victory is complete.

THE CHURCH: THE CORE OF GOD'S KINGDOM ON EARTH

God has a plan for the Church, His Chosen Bride. God is controlling all events, not only on earth but in all the realms—He is the Lord of History and the cosmos. His purpose is to train, grow, and mature us so that we can sit beside His Son and reign and rule with Him.

What does God look like? LOVE.

> *My beloved friends, let us continue to love each other since love comes from God. Everyone who loves is born of God and experiences a relationship with God. The person who refuses to love doesn't know the first thing about God, because God is love—so you can't know him if you don't love. This is how God showed his love for us: God sent his only Son into the world so we might live through him. This is the kind of love we are talking about—not that we once upon a time loved God, but that he loved us and sent his Son as a sacrifice to clear away our sins and the damage they've done to our relationship with God.* (1 John 4:8-10, MSG)

If we, The Church, are to reflect God's light, what should the world see when they look at us? LOVE.

Jesus told us to *"love the Lord our God with all our hearts, all our souls, all our minds, and all our strength."* But He didn't stop there. He told us how to express this kind of Godly love: *"Love our neighbors as ourselves"* (Mark 12:29-31).

This LOVE is expressed in community. And the only way we can live lovingly in community, in unity, is through the Holy Spirit who lives in us (John 17:20-23). Jesus empowered us to bring heaven to earth—to reflect His will and love on earth as it is in heaven. God's kind of love, hesed love, is supernatural, and we are still learning to model His love. The only way we can truly love others—including our enemies and abusers—is by being attached to God, in union with Him through the Holy Spirit.

How will the world know that God loves them? Through the hesed love they see in us—love that is evidence, proof positive that we are His Children, and God is LOVE.

God's Kingdom is more than just a personal experience; it is God's intended will for believers to gather together as The Church. Individually and collectively, we are called to overflow with His love to bring God's Kingdom to earth. And The Church is not an exclusive club—God offers membership to all who believe.

> *The Messiah has made things up between us so that we're now together on this, both non-Jewish outsiders and Jewish insiders. He tore down the wall we used to keep each other at a distance. He repealed the law code that had become so clogged with fine print and footnotes that it hindered more than it helped. Then he started over. Instead of continuing with two groups of people separated by centuries of animosity and suspicion, he created a new kind of human being, a fresh start for everybody.*
>
> *Christ brought us together through his death on the cross. The Cross got us to embrace, and that was the end of the hostility. Christ came and preached peace to you outsiders and peace to us insiders. He treated us as equals, and so made us equals. Through him we both share the same Spirit and have equal access to the Father.* (Ephesians 5:14-18, MSG)

When we climbed on board the "Jesus train," we were joined in an spiritual unity with God (1 Corinthians 6:17). We are reborn as true members of God's family (Ephesians 2:19): children of God

(1 John 5:20). We can escape the destruction of the world and participate in God's divine nature (2 Peter 1:3), and the future starts now with the establishment of God's Kingdom on earth as it is in heaven (1 Peter 1:3). As redeemed humanity, we are destined through our rebirth to reign and rule with Christ (1 Corinthians 6:2).

So, ALL ABOOOARD the Jesus Train. Strike the match with praise, light the fire of faith, pray for God's power to be released so that we can overcome evil and reign and rule with Christ.

Explore and Exercise

1. Heidelberg Catechism Q #32 asks us: "Why we are called Christians?"

   Because by faith I am a member of Christ (1 Corinthians 12:12-27), and so I share in his anointing (1 John 2:27). I am anointed to confess His name (Hebrews 13:15), to present myself to Him as a living sacrifice of thanks (1 Peter 2:5, 9) to strive with a free conscience against sin and the devil in this life (1 Timothy 1:18-19), and afterward to reign with Christ over all creation for eternity (Matthew 25:34).

   a. Explain why progression and transformation as a Christian requires repeating the chorus (emphasizing our main life purpose) over and over again during the songs of our lives.

   b. What does it mean to present ourselves as a living sacrifice of thanks to God?

2. "Be not afraid of discomfort. If you can't put yourself in a situation where you are uncomfortable, then you will never grow. You will never change. You'll never learn." ~ Jason Reynolds, Author

   a. How does Jason Reynolds' quote apply to us as Christians?

   b. Think of a prayer in which you might ask for your own comfort in a specific circumstance (for example: relief from chronic pain or a big bonus on your paycheck).

   c. Using the same situation that you prayed about above, what shape would you have if you asked to be a living sacrifice in that circumstance in order to further the Kingdom of God?

   d. Discuss what internal changes or additions are needed to move from prayer-(b) to prayer-(c), and how would you get there?

Chapter 15: You Just Thank the Lord 209

3. As you read Ephesians 2:6-10 (below), pay attention to the tenses of the underlined verbs.

   ⁶ For he raised us from the dead along with Christ and seated us with him in the heavenly realms because we are united with Christ Jesus. ⁷ So God can point to us in all future ages as examples of the incredible wealth of his grace and kindness toward us, as shown in all he has done for us who are united with Christ Jesus.

   ⁸ God saved you by his grace when you believed. And you can't take credit for this; it is a gift from God. ⁹ Salvation is not a reward for the good things we have done, so none of us can boast about it. ¹⁰ For we are God's masterpiece. He has created us anew in Christ Jesus, so we can do the good things he planned for us long ago. (Ephesians 2:6-10, NLT)

   a. Notice the verbs that are in the past tense (have already happened) in verses 6 and 8: raised, seated, and saved. Explain why the past tense is important to us here.

   b. Look at the verbs in the present tense (now and ongoing) in verse 6 and 10: are united, are, and has created. What significance does the present tense have for believers?

   c. The verb "can" in verse 10 doesn't have all tenses (past, present, and future) that most verbs have, but instead is used to say that someone or something "is able to" do something. What does this verse say we are "made able" to do, and how are we enabled to do this?

4. All of us are called to "spread the good news," to be witnesses who can testify from personal experience about the wonder, majesty, and power of God.

   God sent a man, John the Baptist, to tell about the light so that everyone might believe because of his testimony. John himself was not the light; he was simply a witness to tell about the light. (John 1:6-8, NLT)

   a. How is John the Baptist's life assignment by God similar to our Acts 1:8 mandate?

    b. John was called to preach God's word to the people of his day, comparable to our evangelists or our church's staff workers. Do I have that same calling if I am a truck driver, an accountant, an entrepreneur, a homemaker, or a factory worker? If "yes," how do I do that?

    c. Would an occupation other than church staff relieve me of my responsibility to testify? Explain your answer.

5. **Reign and Rule Challenge.** So who is standing against Satan's total rule in human affairs? We are: you and I, as individual Christians and corporately, as the Church. If we look at history with all our shortcomings, weaknesses, and appalling failures, we might throw up our hands in despair. The fight would be hopeless if it was only puny humans in the fight, but we are the Church of the Living God! If God is for us, who can stand against us (2 Chronicles 20:6)?

    a. Remember that you and I are the Church. Read the passages below. Pay attention to the resources God makes available to us as individual Christians and as a believing church.

We know that none of the God-born makes a practice of sin—fatal sin. The God-born are also the God-protected. The Evil One can't lay a hand on them. We know that we are held firm by God; it's only the people of the world who continue in the grip of the Evil One. And we know that the Son of God came so we could recognize and understand the truth of God—what a gift!—and we are living in the Truth itself, in God's Son, Jesus Christ. This Jesus is both True God and Real Life. (1 John 5:18-20, MSG)

My response is to get down on my knees before the Father, this magnificent Father who parcels out all heaven and earth. I ask him to strengthen you by his Spirit—not a brute strength but a glorious inner strength—that Christ will live in you as you open the door and invite him in. And I ask him that with both feet planted firmly on love, you'll be able to take in with all followers of Jesus the extravagant dimensions of Christ's love. Reach out and experience the breadth! Test its length! Plumb the depths!

Rise to the heights! Live full lives, full in the fullness of God. (Ephesians 3:14-19, MSG)

   b. As you live your life right now, in the place and time where God has placed you, what opportunities are available to you to be an ambassador for the Kingdom of God (2 Corinthians 5:17-21)? What could this look like?

PART 5: CHAPTER 16

Bear Fruit in the Kingdom of God

For the Kingdom of God is not just a lot of talk; it is living by God's power.
(1 Corinthians 4:20, NLT)

God established a covenant with His people and sealed it with a sign. Our God is intent on keeping His covenant.

> *Then God said, "When I see the rainbow in the clouds, I will remember the eternal covenant between God and every living creature on earth."* (Genesis 9:16. NLT)

As a young reader of fantasy, I, Kathleen, made a connection in my mind with the mythical pot of gold hidden at the end of the rainbow and God's promises. Adventurers were always chasing after leprechauns' treasure. It became an obsession and a driving force in their lives, because if they found the gold, they would be set for life. Now, each time I see a rainbow, I am reminded of God's promises which I visualize as my pot of gold. The great adventure of my life is to seek after God and His Kingdom, and I've found the gold! And I'm not only set for life, but for eternity. So are you.

God made over 7,000 promises to His people in the Bible. Just a few are listed here:

- Adoption (John 1:12)
- Eternal life (John 3:16)
- Full life (John 10:10)
- Holy Spirit (Acts 1:8)
- Guidance (John 16:13)
- Divine Healing (James 5:14-15)
- Rescue (Psalm 34:19

- Provision (Philippians 4:19)
- Answered prayer (Mark 11:24)
- Anything is possible (Mark 9:23-24)
- God insures our good (Romans 8:28)
- Grace (2 Corinthians 12:9)
- Peace (Isaiah 26:3-4)
- Rest from our labors (Hebrews 4:9-11)
- Eternity with God (John 14:1-6)
- All promises fulfilled (2 Corinthians 1:20)

God gave us a rainbow as a sign of His covenant with us. It's visible. It's real. Even those who haven't yet committed to God can see it in the sky and be awed by its beauty. God made promises to us that He will keep—for eternity.

As we draw closer and closer to God, as we make a habit of looping through the chain reaction of praise, we move into lives that are transformative and authentic. What signs of the covenant with our Holy Father can people see if they scrutinize our lives—are there signs of the riches we enjoy? Jesus lived His life in plain sight for all to see. People flocked to Him in response to the signs and wonders that they saw; these signs provided evidence that God was with Him (John 2:23). This pattern was also evident in the spread of Christianity as described in the Book of Acts: people were attracted by signs and wonders and stayed to hear the Gospel.

LIVING IN THE KINGDOM OF GOD

WE DISPLAY THE BEATITUDES IN OUR LIVES. Huge crowds followed Jesus constantly—following the miracles, the signs and wonders, and wondering who this man really was. In Matthew 5:1-16, we read that Jesus climbed a hillside, and only those who were really committed followers made the steep climb after him. Arriving at a suitable quiet place, Jesus sat down and taught those who had made the effort, climbed the hill, to hear what He had to say. This teaching is commonly known as "The Sermon on the Mount: The Beatitudes."

Each beatitude begins with the Greek word *makarios* which means "blessed are" and embraces more than just the emotional state of happiness. It includes spiritual well-being and the approval of God, which is the first taste of life eternal—God's Kingdom on earth. As we live in the truth of the Beatitudes, we reflect the Holy Spirit who lives in us. Let's examine this new life in Christ.

Blessed are the poor in spirit, for theirs is the kingdom of heaven (Matthew 5:3). We understand that material poverty is the lack of even the most basic resources; this is also true for us spiritually. When we are brought to the end of ourselves and realize our great spiritual need (become poor in spirit), we recognize our need for and dependence on God alone.

Blessed are those who mourn, for they will be comforted (Matthew 5:4). We are often filled with grief over sin and evil, especially our own, and mourn over the failure of mankind to give proper glory to God. Our pain-filled lamentations begin our 180-degree pivot away from the world and toward God. In His arms, we are comforted and renewed so that we can follow the way of God in righteousness as we live in the Kingdom of God on earth.

Blessed are the meek [also translated humble or gentle], *for they will inherit the earth* (Matthew 5:5). Meekness is an attitude of humility and submission to God as we follow the pattern of Jesus. The Greek word for meek, *praus*, was borrowed from the military and relates to horse training. A horse that is "gentled" submits to the rider. Even though it might want to gallop, it trots or walks at the master's will and command. The horse submits all that it is and has to the master. The same Greek word is translated as "gentle" in Matthew 11:29 when Jesus tells his disciples to *"take my yoke upon you,"* to obey the will of God. God's promise of inheritance is explained in Romans 4:13 and Hebrews 11:16.

Blessed are those who hunger and thirst for righteousness, for they will be filled (Matthew 5:6). When you are really hungry, food has a special flavor and is especially satisfying. Imagine the hunger pangs of a first century Palestinian laborer who often went without food for extended periods of time. Imagine the thirst from laboring in the heat of the desert. Those who seek God's righteousness—in the same way the desert laborer desired food and drink—receive what they desire.

Blessed are the merciful, for they will be shown mercy (Matthew 5:7). Mercy is the benevolent nature of love and empathy for those who suffer. Mercy is what God has given us, and it is what we are to offer to others (Matthew 18:21-35).

Blessed are the pure in heart, for they will see God Matthew 5:8). Rather than living out of selfish purposes and self-seeking motives, we are to willingly serve and sacrifice for others, just as Jesus did for us. In the NOW of the Kingdom of God, we "see" God through the eyes of faith; when the NOT YET Kingdom appears, we shall "see Christ as he is" (1 John 3:2).

Blessed are the peacemakers, for they will be called children of God (Matthew 5:9). Love unites; hate divides. A peacemaker is one who strives to maintain a genuine harmony among people. A true peacemaker is an instrument in the hands of Christ; she is one who cultivates hearts of peace between God and herself and shares this peace with others, even her enemies (Matthew 5:43-44).

Blessed are those who are persecuted because of righteousness, for theirs is the kingdom of heaven (Matthew 5:10). Jesus said many times that those who follow Him will be mistreated as He was (John 15:20-21). But we also participate in His victory: even if we are wrongfully mistreated here on earth as a result of our belief or devotion to God, we shall be blessed eternally in the Kingdom of Heaven. **Oppression on account of our faith in Christ draws us out of the noise of the world and wraps us in the profound rest of His other-worldly silence and peace.**

If you have been drawing up a "to-do list" for life as you read through the beatitudes, guess what? We can't accomplish this kind of living no matter how eagerly we "keep the rules." But with the Holy Spirit living inside us, with habits of praise that bring our focus to Father God, we are being transformed into the character of Jesus—Jesus lived the beatitudes.

WE ARE RENEWED AND TRANSFORMED. To Paul's Roman audience (Romans 12:1-2), the idea of "sacrifice" was often synonymous with religion. When you sinned, you brought an animal to the temple to be killed as payment for your sins. When you sinned again, you sacrificed another animal. This often led to abuses of the system because people thought that all they had to do to satisfy or appease their God was to offer the required sacrifice. Sincerity or change of heart didn't necessarily come into play.

So Paul introduced a new kind of sacrifice—one of our living selves: *consider yourselves to be dead to the power of sin and alive to God through Christ Jesus* (Hebrews 6:11). This calls for a change in who we are inside. We put to death (sacrifice) our own self-focused sinful nature because we understand Jesus' grace and its place in our lives. We offer ourselves intelligently and willingly, not ignorantly like animals brought to slaughter, but by choosing God, transforming our minds, so that we can follow the will of God. This new orientation in our thinking leads to a new direction in our behavior.

> *Since you have heard about Jesus and have learned the truth that comes from him, throw off your old sinful nature and your former way of life, which is corrupted by lust and deception. Instead, let the Spirit renew your thoughts and attitudes. Put on your new nature, created to be like God—truly righteous and holy.* (Ephesians 4:21-24, NLT)

What does this look like? It's a two-part process, like refinishing furniture or flipping houses. Specific demolition comes first—remove the old so that it can be replaced with the new. We choose to replace lies with truth, swap cultural influence for God's mindset, gain control over anger, work willingly to honor God, and be kind to each other, tenderhearted, forgiving one another, just as God through Christ has forgiven you (Ephesians 4: 32). We are renewed.

GOD'S LOVE IS EVIDENT BY THE FRUITS WE BEAR. Any farmer or gardener will tell you that the health and contribution of a plant is demonstrated by the fruit it produces. Paul used the metaphor of fruit in his letter to the Galatians, possibly drawn from Isaiah (Isaiah 32:15-17) as well as Jesus' teaching.

> *But the Holy Spirit produces this kind of fruit in our lives: love, joy, peace, patience, kindness, goodness, faithfulness, gentleness, and self-control. There is no law against these things!* (Galatians 5:22-26, NLT)

The genuineness of Christ followers—of us—will be demonstrated by good fruit we produce in our lives. However, bearing fruit is not the same thing as earning "heaven points" through doing righteous works—we can't earn our faith by trying harder. We can bear fruit only when we submit to the Holy Spirit as our gardener: weeding, pruning, feeding, and encouraging. We ask Him to expose, dig out, and transform everything that is not God in us.

Paul ends his letter to the Galatians by warning them that evil also bears fruit—of the worm-filled, rotten variety—so we need to be careful which garden we are tending.

> *Do not be deceived: God cannot be mocked. A man reaps what he sows. Whoever sows to please their flesh, from the flesh will reap destruction; whoever sows to please the Spirit, from the Spirit will reap eternal life.* (Galatians 6:7-8, NIV)

Jesus taught that the presence of the Spirit and communion with Him is what produces the fruits of love and obedience, so **the possibility of life in the Kingdom of God is not one of human responsibility, but it is one of divine enablement** (John 14-15). The Holy Spirit produces these fruits in us, and Christ-followers must choose to open their hearts and let the Spirit be operative in our lives.

Let's look at the fruits of the Spirit compared with their antitheses (the works of the flesh).

- **Love** vs Hatred

    Love is dominant, listed first, because all of the Holy Spirit fruits flow out of love.

- **Joy** vs Conflict

    Joy flows out of healthy relationships; broken relationships build bitterness and anger.

- **Peace** vs Discord

    Peace arises as we lovingly serve each other, producing harmony and order. Self-focus disrupts.

- **Patience** vs Rage

    Patience is the quality of staying the course in spite of being wronged or irritated.

- **Kindness** and **Goodness** vs Enmity

    Kindness and goodness, together with patience, enable us to respond lovingly toward those around us even when wronged.

- **Faithful** vs Erratic

    Only through the Holy Spirit can we produce steadfast loyalty in our attitudes and relationships.

- **Gentleness** vs Selfish Ambition

    Gentleness is the humble attitude that considers the needs and hurts of others before one's personal goals.

- **Self-Control** vs Selfish Indulgence

    Self-control, which is really "Holy-Spirit-enabled control," gives us the strength to say "no" to the desires of our sinful natures and choose another path.

IMITATE JESUS CHRIST

BE HUMBLE. Pride is the opposite of humility, and it is tied up with our ego. As soldiers engaged in spiritual battle, pride is often our major battleground. The devil would love for us to forget that our fruits are divinely-enabled and fill us with a false chain reaction of pride, self-contentment, egocentricity, judgement of others, conflict, hatred, and chaos. When we embrace the self-importance of our sinful nature, our Holy-Spirit-fruit degrade to become the devil's false and worm-infested replicas. We proudly think we can earn our way to heaven through works, and so, full of pride, we lose the battle which Jesus Christ already won for us. And the devil laughs.

BE WORTHY OF THE GOSPEL OF CHRIST (Philippians 1:27). Paul's letter to the church at Philippi is a call to humility for all Christ-followers as individuals and as a body—the church. You can see the beatitudes and the fruits of the Spirit at work in the picture of The Church that Paul paints.

Encourage Each Other in Christ.

- DO. *If you've gotten anything at all out of following Christ, if his love has made any difference in your life, if being in a community of the Spirit means anything to you, if you have a heart, if you care—then do me a favor: Agree with each other, love each other, be deep-spirited friends.* (Philippians 2:1, MSG)

- DON'T. *Don't push your way to the front; don't sweet-talk your way to the top. Put yourself aside, and help others get ahead. Don't be obsessed with getting your own advantage. Forget yourselves long enough to lend a helping hand.* (Philippians 2:2, MSG)

Eliminate Your Pride; Replace It with Fellowship.

- DO. *Think of yourselves the way Christ Jesus thought of himself. He had equal status with God but didn't think so much of himself that he had to cling to the advantages of that status no matter what. Not at all. When the time came, he set aside the privileges of deity and took on the status of a slave, became human! Having become human, he stayed human. It was an incredibly humbling process. He didn't claim special privileges. Instead, he lived a selfless, obedient life and then died a selfless, obedient death—and the worst kind of death at that—a crucifixion.* (Philippians 2:5-8, MSG)

- DON'T. *Don't claim special privileges.* (Philippians 2:7, MSG)

Rejoice Together with Lives of Responsive Obedience.

- DO. *What I'm getting at, friends, is that you should simply keep on doing what you've done from the beginning... Keep it up. Better yet, redouble your efforts. Be energetic in your life of salvation, reverent and sensitive before God. That energy is God's energy, an energy deep within you, God himself willing and working at what will give him the most pleasure.* (Philippians 2:12-13, MSG)

- DON'T. *Do everything without complaining and arguing.* (Philippians 2:14, NLT)

- DO. *Go out into the world uncorrupted, a breath of fresh air in this squalid and polluted society. Provide people with a glimpse of good living and of the living God. Carry the light-giving Message into the night so I'll have good cause to be proud of you on the day that Christ returns.* (Philippians 2:15-16, MSG)

Let's make church a four-letter word: LOVE. We are Christ-followers. We know that The Word become flesh and blood (human) and moved into our neighborhood on earth. We have seen His one-of-a-kind glory; we have been received in the Circle of Love; we are part of His family.

But whoever did want him, who believed he was who he claimed and would do what he said, He made to be their true selves, their child-of-God selves. These are the God-begotten, not blood-begotten, not flesh-begotten, not sex-begotten. (John 1:12-13, MSG)

We are The Church, and our mission is to reveal The Kingdom of God to the world. In ongoing relationship with God, we open ourselves up to the Gospel message, hear the Holy Spirit's knock, and throw wide the doors to our hearts. In turn, the Holy Spirit enables us to bear fruit and obediently live out the Beatitudes. **We are a renewed, transformed, holy people who reflect God's love to the world.**

Take time every day, every hour, every minute, to pause and let go. The journey of transformation is yours to take…Let your heart and eyes open to the wonder of being a son and daughter of the Father. Taste now and see that He is so very good. Not of this world, you are now called to shine within it with a light that is also not of this world.

> Let the Kingdom of God, the realm of heaven, Christ Himself, be released from within you to love the world around you. In this way His Kingdom comes. His will is done, on earth as it is in heaven.
> ~ Ted Dekker, The Forgotten Way Study Guide, Outlaw Studios, 2015, p158

Explore and Exercise

1. *And the city has no need of sun or moon, for the glory of God illuminates the city, and the Lamb is its light.* (Revelation 21:23, NLT)

   "You are the light of the world—like a city on a hilltop that cannot be hidden. No one lights a lamp and then puts it under a basket. Instead, a lamp is placed on a stand, where it gives light to everyone in the house. In the same way, let your good deeds shine out for all to see, so that everyone will praise your heavenly Father. (Matthew 5:14-16, NLT)

   a. How do these verses speak into who God made us to be and what our purpose is here on earth?

   b. What kind of situations make you wish you could hide under a basket instead standing on a platform for all to see? In other words, where do you struggle most with allowing the temptations and values of the world to unplug you from the source of light inside you?

   c. **Personal Reign and Rule Challenge.** Make a personal God-chart that speaks especially into this "hiding-under-a-basket" area. List promises and reminders to help you progress through praise > faith > prayer > overcoming evil > so that you can reign and rule with Christ as a lamp on a stand that gives light to everyone in the house.

2. "God's Kingdom on Earth—He's got to be kidding! The earth is a zoo, a madhouse, an explosion waiting to happen!"

   Most of us have experienced the frustration of be faced with what can seem to be an impossible task—being "God imagers" who reflect His love to those around us. But we are not without resources.

   a. Share a Biblical or modern-day story that demonstrates Holy Spirit power or renewal that make it possible to overcome evil and bring God's light to earth.

b. Do you have a personal experience of when the Lord used you to bring heaven to earth?

3. Choose one of the Beatitudes from Jesus' Sermon on the Mount in Matthew and give a modern-day example of what this could look like in the world today.

4. "You Christians think you can do something wrong, say, 'Oops, sorry,' and all is forgiven. So you can do whatever you want and all is forgiven."

   a. Read Romans 6:1-14. How would you answer this accusation?

   b. How would you explain "putting on a new nature" or transformation? What does love have to do with it?

   c. Is there a difference between being a philanthropist and displaying the fruits of the Spirit? Explain.

5. To "reign and rule with Christ" is a Christian phrase that can be very confusing, even to some Christians, but definitely to nonbelievers. How would you explain that concept? Write out an explanation so that you will be ready with an answer when questioned. You may want to draw on Ephesians 1:9-11 and Romans 8:9-11 (below).

   God has now revealed to us his mysterious will regarding Christ—which is to fulfill his own good plan. And this is the plan: At the right time he will bring everything together under the authority of Christ—everything in heaven and on earth. Furthermore, because we are united with Christ, we have received an inheritance from God, for he chose us in advance, and he makes everything work out according to his plan. (Ephesians 1:9-11, NLT)

   But if God himself has taken up residence in your life, you can hardly be thinking more of yourself than of him. Anyone, of course, who has not welcomed this invisible but clearly present God, the Spirit of Christ, won't know what we're talking about. But for you who welcome him, in whom he dwells—even though you still experience all the limitations of sin—you yourself experience life on God's terms. It stands to reason, doesn't it, that if the alive-and-present God who raised Jesus from the dead moves into your life, he'll do the same thing in you that he did in Jesus, bringing you alive to himself? When God lives and breathes in you (and he does, as surely as he did in Jesus), you are delivered from that dead life. With his Spirit living in you, your body will be as alive as Christ's! (Romans 8:9-11, MSG)

6. **Reign and Rule Challenge.** We sing songs that say, "More of You, and less of me," asking for God to renew us, to help us tear out our sin nature by the roots and replace it with His character of love. This is something we cannot do in our own strength; God knows that and has made provision for that as well—the Holy Spirit dwells in each of us.

   God has also set up a system of working with His people: we pray; He responds. So as we seek God and His Kingdom here on earth, we pray for His love to shine through us visible by the fruits we bear. And they are not our fruits, but fruits of the Spirit.

   Use the "Fruit-of-the-Spirit prayers" below as templates for your own prayers. Seek God's help as you ask Him to fill you so full of the His Fruit that they will be evident in your life, in your family, in your church, in your community. Thy Kingdom come, Thy will be done, on earth as it is in heaven.

   a. Lord, I open my heart and soul up to you as soil cultivated by the Master Gardener. Help me to cooperate with the Holy Spirit, to submit to Your pruning, to grow in the shape that You have for me. Lord, I look to You as the source of all I need—Son light, Living Water, and Bread of Life. Help me grow where You have planted me so that I can **share your good fruit**. Amen.

   b. God, You are **love**. Let me be a reflection of You, remembering that no occasion, hurt, or injustice justifies hatred or bitterness. Let me love like Jesus loves. Let me love who Jesus loves. Amen.

c. Lord, let your **joy** fill me so full that it splashes on all those around me. This joy can be playful, quiet, tearful, raucous, or dancing, but never cynical, lazy, selfish, or disdainful. When problems block my way, let me see past these barriers. From the depths of the joy I have in You, help me to view difficulties as opportunities to see You at work in my life and in the lives of those around me. Amen.

d. Father in heaven, thank for your gifts of mercy, grace, and salvation. I live forgiven. With your strength and power, I will also forgive others so that I may live. **All peace** comes from You, and I praise You for this blessing. Amen.

e. Lord, inconveniences seemed to be the order of the day today, and I ran out of **patience** before noon. Tear these impatient weeds from my heart, so that I don't curse those who push me, delay me, or take my place. Instead, Lord, my prayer is that in your strength I can unclench my fists, quiet my irritation, accept your love-filled fruit in its place, and display it with courage. Amen.

f. Jesus Christ, help my **kindness** to reflect yours—to all those around me. Help me to be kind even when it will not be given back to me in return. Like you, I want to be kind to the rich and poor, the lonely and gregarious, the nice and mean, and the deserving and undeserving. Let me treat others in the way you have treated me. Amen.

g. Jesus, help me to reflect your **goodness**, not with pride as a goody-two-shoes would, but with a humble servant spirit. May every dollar I take in be honestly earned and may every advance come from my own honest labor. Dear Lord, convict me to confess before I accuse. With your Holy Spirit whispering in my heart, may I choose goodness. Amen.

h. Father God, take the ax to my selfish desires and pleasures; replace them with **faithfulness**. Help me to keep my promises, repay my debts, live up to my word, and love always, starting at home and offering the fruit of love to all who I come in contact with. You have promised faithfulness to generations of those who love You and serve You. Help my life to model Your faithfulness. Amen.

i. Lord, I ask you to help me to comprehend that **gentleness** is not the opposite of strength, but requires me to be filled with Your power. Give me the gentleness of eternity because You have shown me that nothing will be won there by using force here on earth. Let my voice be raised only in praise and my hands clenched only in prayer. May I walk in Your footsteps, covered with the dust of Your gentle Spirit. Amen.

j. Holy Spirit, be my General so I may march as a soldier obeying your orders for **self-control**. There is a constant war within myself—sin vs. Your character—and I need Your strong commands. I rejoice that I am a spiritual being, and when this body is dead, You have promised that my spirit will soar for eternity. Amen.

k. Master Gardener, thank you for cultivating, pruning, and weeding the garden that is me. I commit myself to bearing Your fruits: **love, joy, peace, patience, kindness, goodness faithfulness, gentleness, and self-control.** When my fruit is nutritious and bountiful, I will give You thanks. If the fruit I bear is worm-eaten and rotten, I will pray for Your amazing grace. And each night, may I sleep peacefully, knowing that your mercies are new every morning. Amen.

CHAPTER 17

God's Provision: A Chain Reaction

The Bible has not only given us the beginning and the ending, but it gives us a pathway that leads us through the sometimes murky and dangerous middle.

Chain Reaction of Praise

The Bible's awesome conclusion—the NOT YET Kingdom of God—is described in the Book of Revelation. The Garden of Eden relationship with God that mankind lost in Genesis is rediscovered in the Bible's last chapter as evil is finally overcome. Monsters from the earth, the sea, and the pit fall before the Lamb who had already been slaughtered, but returned to glorious life. The wicked are barred from New Jerusalem, but believers are invited to repent, wash their robes, and enter through the city gates that will never be shut (Revelation 21:25).

> Then God said, "It's happened. I'm A to Z. I'm the Beginning, I'm the Conclusion. From Water-of-Life Well I give freely to the thirsty. Conquerors inherit all this. I'll be God to them, they'll be sons and daughters to me. (Revelation 21: 6-7, MSG)

This is what God has promised those who believe in Him—eternity in a city *that doesn't need sun or moon for light. God's Glory is its light, the Lamb its lamp! The nations will walk in its light ... and there won't be any night* (Revelation 21:23).

A close and abiding relationship with mankind was God's intentional will when He created us. Despite our fall into sin, His ultimate will remains the same—eternal association with us in heaven—and the Good News of Jesus Christ is the pathway that makes it possible. To the world, Calvary is considered defeat and Satan the victor, but they miss the conclusive triumph of the resurrection.

> *For he raised us from the dead along with Christ and seated us with him in the heavenly realms because we are united with Christ Jesus. So God can point to us in all future ages as examples of the incredible wealth of his grace and kindness toward us, as shown in all he has done for us who are united with Christ Jesus.* (Ephesians 2:6-7, NLT)

Those of us reading this book are living in God's NOW Kingdom on earth as we look forward to the NOT YET fully revealed heavenly realm, but God has not only promised and provided a certain future, He is taking care of all the present details through the Holy Spirit who equips us to battle evil and establish the Kingdom of God here. This was God's plan from the beginning of humanity: being in relationship with us.

God chooses to conduct business with His people by walking side-by-side, carrying us when necessary, and giving us assistance as we limp or stumble. And we can choose: to spend time alone with Him, sit down at the dinner table with Him, praise and worship Him, and throw open the door to our hearts when He knocks. We can also choose not to open the door; that's entirely up to us.

> *Don't look for shortcuts to God. The market is flooded with surefire, easygoing formulas for a successful life that can be practiced in your spare time. Don't fall for that stuff, even though crowds of people do. The way to life—to God!—is vigorous and requires total attention.* (Matthew 7:13-14, MSG)

CHAIN REACTION

The Bible has not only given us the beginning and the ending, it gives us a pathway that leads us through the sometimes murky and dangerous middle. To enable us to live in Kingdom of God on earth, the Bible gives us a chain reaction, a loop that keeps us in God's Circle of Love in the present.

"Chain Reaction" is a scientific term for a sequence of reactions where the reactive product or byproduct causes additional reactions to take place. In other words, one thing leads to another.

PRAISE begins the loop that draws us forward into the Kingdom of God. As we focus on the truth of who God is and our covenantal relationship to Him, the radical effect that blooms inside us erases Satan's efforts to get believers to forget that we are risen and exalted with Christ (1 John 5:18).

FAITH is the reactive byproduct of praise, so when the devil's ploys dampen faith's flames, we can strike the match of praise. God gave each of us just the amount of faith that we need; it is always within reach despite the roadblocks and barriers set by the evil one (Romans 12:6). In the battle to choose faith, praise is our mighty weapon of choice, and it is a choice we must make daily.

PRAYER is the God-designed system through which He releases His power to the world. The decisions are made in heaven: We pray; He responds. Jesus modeled this for us as He prayed in the Garden of Gethsemane for release from suffering. "Yet I want your will to be done, not mine" (Mark 14:36). The battle was fought during Thursday's prayer in the olive grove—that's when victory was achieved. Friday and Saturday were just getting the job done; Jesus won the battle by praying for God's power in an olive grove.

We can't **OVERCOME EVIL** from the bleacher seats, we need to put on the Armor of God and jump into action. Our armor needs constant replenishment, which happens as we praise God, stand in faith, and pray for God's power. To overcome evil takes spiritual exercise, training, and persistence in walking closely with God, and He gives us all the authority and resources we need to join the battle. Jesus Christ has already assured the final victory.

As grace-equipped people, we **REIGN AND RULE WITH CHRIST** on earth and for eternity (1 Peter 1:3-5). Jesus' prayer in John 17 gives us a picture of how this is possible:

Father, I want those you gave me to be with me, right where I am, so they can see my glory, the splendor you gave me, having loved me long before there ever was a world. Righteous Father, the world has never known you, but I have known you, and these disciples know that you sent me on this mission. I have made your very being known to them—who you are and what you do—and continue to make it known, so that your love for me might be in them exactly as I am in them. (John 17:24-26. MSG)

Praise is the vital beginning of this chain reaction. It is the match that ignites our faith. As our faith flames and our connection with the Holy Spirit strengthens, we learn to pray prayers for God's power to overcome evil. This chain reaction isn't a once-and-done occurrence, but a loop-de-loop that we reprise over and over again, like the chorus of a song. And it is in the Circle of Love that we experience glimmers of our destination—reigning and ruling with Christ—along the journey.

LIFE IN THE "NOW" KINGDOM OF GOD

Since the third century, the church had been given a voice in the center of Western Culture. But we Christians now live in a post-Christian world. Even so, we will not live as victims in exile, but as victorious conquerors in Christ Jesus. The Kingdom of God is still strongly evident here on earth in His Bride, the church. Jesus endured unspeakable horrors to save us—that's how much He loves us—and that beauty-out-of-horror continues. God brings all things together for good for those of us who love him and are called according to His purpose (Romans 8:28).

It is walking with God that enables us to have beautiful relationships with others—this beauty draws others to the gospel like moths the light. It is seen in the power of prayer to change things. It is seen in Holy Spirit weapons that overcome evil.

We have a beautiful gospel, a brilliant light in the darkness, a lovely fragrance that dispels odor, and faith-filled actions that overflow with His love. This is His Kingdom NOW, exiled but still present in a broken world. This is His Kingdom NOT YET which is ours for eternity.

These words of encouragement from the Book of Jude are for all of us who love the Lord.

But you, dear friends, carefully build yourselves up in this most holy faith by praying in the Holy Spirit, staying right at the center of God's love, keeping your arms open and outstretched, ready for the mercy of our Master, Jesus Christ. This is the unending life, the real life! Go easy on those who hesitate in the faith. Go after those who take the wrong way. Be tender with sinners, but not soft on sin. The sin itself stinks to high heaven.

And now to him who can keep you on your feet, standing tall in his bright presence, fresh and celebrating—to our one God, our only Savior, through Jesus Christ, our Master, be glory, majesty, strength, and rule before all time, and now, and to the end of all time. Yes. (Jude 1:20-25, MSG)

Explore and Exercise

1. We don't need to be discouraged or afraid to face the evil in our lives, our families, our communities, our countries, and our world. God has laid out a road map to prepare us, to engage with us, and to protect us as we engage in the battle. Read Colossians 3:1-17 together.

    1-2 So if you're serious about living this new resurrection life with Christ, act like it. Pursue the things over which Christ presides. Don't shuffle along, eyes to the ground, absorbed with the things right in front of you. Look up, and be alert to what is going on around Christ—that's where the action is. See things from his perspective.

    3-4 Your old life is dead. Your new life, which is your real life—even though invisible to spectators—is with Christ in God. He is your life. When Christ (your real life, remember) shows up again on this earth, you'll show up, too—the real you, the glorious you. Meanwhile, be content with obscurity, like Christ.

    5-8 And that means killing off everything connected with that way of death: sexual promiscuity, impurity, lust, doing whatever you feel like whenever you feel like it, and grabbing whatever attracts your fancy. That's a life shaped by things and feelings instead of by God. It's because of this kind of thing that God is about to explode in anger. It wasn't long ago that you were doing all that stuff and not knowing any better. But you know better now, so make sure it's all gone for good: bad temper, irritability, meanness, profanity, dirty talk.

    9-11 Don't lie to one another. You're done with that old life. It's like a filthy set of ill-fitting clothes you've stripped off and put in the fire. Now you're dressed in a new wardrobe. Every item of your new way of life is custom-made by the Creator, with his label on it. All the old fashions are now obsolete. Words like Jewish and non-Jewish, religious and irreligious, insider and outsider, uncivilized and uncouth, slave and free, mean nothing. From now on everyone is defined by Christ, everyone is included in Christ.

Chapter 17: God's Provision: A Chain Reaction   235

> *¹²⁻¹⁴ So, chosen by God for this new life of love, dress in the wardrobe God picked out for you: compassion, kindness, humility, quiet strength, discipline. Be even-tempered, content with second place, quick to forgive an offense. Forgive as quickly and completely as the Master forgave you. And regardless of what else you put on, wear love. It's your basic, all-purpose garment. Never be without it.*
>
> *¹⁵⁻¹⁷ Let the peace of Christ keep you in tune with each other, in step with each other. None of this going off and doing your own thing. And cultivate thankfulness. Let the Word of Christ—the Message—have the run of the house. Give it plenty of room in your lives. Instruct and direct one another using good common sense. And sing, sing your hearts out to God! Let every detail in your lives—words, actions, whatever—be done in the name of the Master, Jesus, thanking God the Father every step of the way.* (Colossian 3:1-17, MSG)

a. Identify the places in this passage where you can find the steps of the chain reaction:

   i. Strike the match: praise God in all circumstances

   ii. To ignite and flame your faith,

   iii. So that you can pray for God's power and authority

   iv. To overcome evil.

   v. Reign and Rule with Christ NOW.

b. Share some examples of how you have used (or you could use) the chain progression in your life. You might think of an emotion or situation that makes you feel separate from God or remember a real-life experience that filled you with fear or doubt. How might the chain progression make a difference?

c. Is learning about this chain reaction enough? After all, you've read the book, taken the class, and received your diploma, so does that not mean you are set for life? You might find the foundation for your answer in Colossians 3 that we just studied (above). Share why we will continue to use these steps as we move from this life to eternity. Will any part of the chain reaction become unnecessary?

Appendices

We taught this material with a test class, and we spent time reviewing some Biblical concepts during class time that are the foundational material of our faith. For that reason, we chose to give simple explanations on these subjects as appendices:

- The Circle of Love
- The Order of Salvation
- The Will of God

For those interested in being the point person for a groups study of this book, Appendix B provides some suggestions and helpful information.

- Leader Guide
- Video Introductions. Six short introductory videos by the authors are available for purchase (download) on www.kathleensevenhouse.com

APPENDIX A
The Circle of Love

Enter the Circle of Love and become like our Triune God—belong to each other, be one as our God is one, refuse to live our lives alone, and intentionally invite others in to the wonder of this Circle.

The simple drawing below represents God as the Trinity: Father, Son, and Holy Spirit. Although the word "Trinity" isn't used in the Bible, God gives us a clear picture of Himself as a relational being—Father, Son, and Holy Spirit—who is never alone in all of eternity. He is One God in three personages who are united in fellowship with each other. Mark 1:9-12 reveals the intimacy, identity, and belonging of the Father, Son, and Holy Spirit. And through Jesus Christ, we are invited to be a part of the family circle.

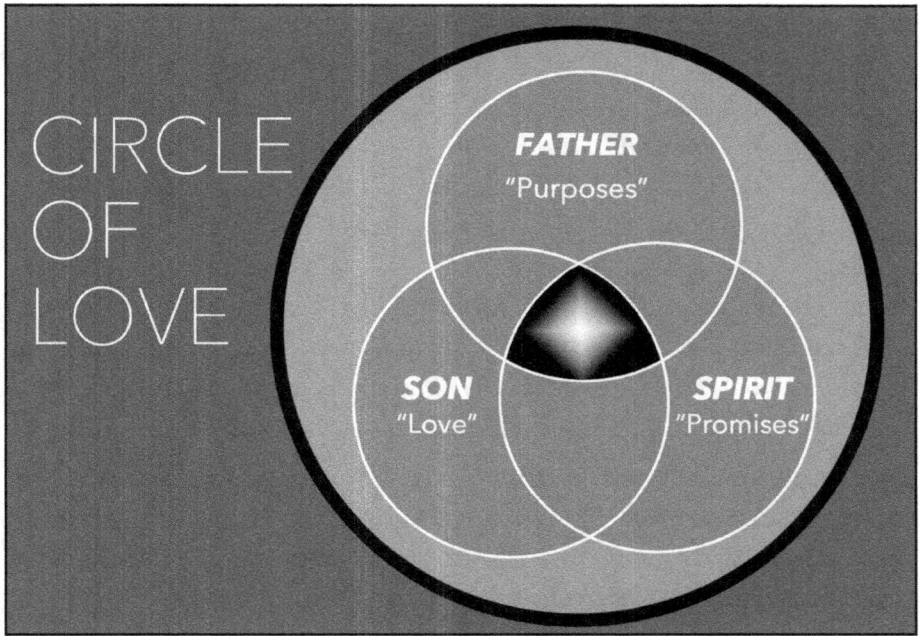

Throughout *Strike the Match, Light the Fire*, we refer to our relationship with God as being invited into His family, to being adopted into true fellowship, to living with God in this Circle of Love, both in this life and the life to come. We were created for this relationship (Ephesians 1:4-5), made in the image of God's community, with a deep longing to love and to be loved.

The kind of love that God has for humanity comes from the Greek word *agapē* and means "an unconditional love that wills to live for the good of another." John 3:16-17 are verses that are often used to summarize the Gospel message of love.

> *For this is how God loved the world: He gave his one and only Son, so that everyone who believes in him will not perish but have eternal life. God sent his Son into the world not to judge the world, but to save the world through him.* (John 3:16-17, NLT)

Jesus' prayer in John 15 illustrates the love and connection of the Trinity and how all believers are invited to dwell and remain in the Circle of Love (John 15:9-10), so that God's people may be one as we are one (John 15:11). Jesus continued to pray for His disciples and all who believe in Him:

> *My prayer is not for them alone. I pray for those who will believe in me through their message, that all of them may be one, Father, just as you are in me and I am in you. May they also be in us so that the world may believe that you have sent me. I have given them the glory that you gave me, that they may be one as we are one—I in them and you in me—so that they may be brought to complete unity. Then the world will know that you sent me and have loved them even as you have loved me...I have made you known to them, and will continue to make you known in order that the love you have for me may be in them and that I myself may be in them.* (John 15:2-24, 26, NIV)

Our understanding of God is the most important thing about us. Is God trustworthy? Does my image of God instill confidence and hope? Am I seen, heard, felt, and loved by God? When we realize we can't be separated from God (Romans 8:38-39), that we are chosen, loved, called, and adopted into His family (Ephesians 1:3-5), it changes how we think, how we live, and who we are—we become Jesus-minded (Philippians 2).

Appendix A: The Circle of Love

We are living in the Circle of Love right now, in a world driven by power, greed, and hatred. Jesus taught us to pray, "Thy Kingdom come on earth as it is in heaven," and His Kingdom is here as we surrender to God and remain in His Circle. Then we are able to bring His Kingdom to those around us on earth. And we will need courage.

> *So be truly glad. There is wonderful joy ahead, even though you must endure many trials for a little while. These trials will show that your faith is genuine. It is being tested as fire tests and purifies gold—though your faith is far more precious than mere gold. So, when your faith remains strong through many trials, it will bring you much praise and glory and honor on the day when Jesus Christ is revealed to the whole world.* (1 Peter 1:6-7, NLT)

God has a purpose for us on this earth, both as individuals and kingdom dwellers (Jeremiah 29:11-12).

> *Build houses and settle down; plant gardens and eat what they produce. Marry and have sons and daughters; find wives for your sons and give your daughters in marriage, so that they too may have sons and daughters. Increase in number there; do not decrease. Also, seek the peace and prosperity of the city to which I have carried you into exile. Pray to the Lord for it, because if it prospers, you too will prosper.* (Jeremiah 29:5-7)

So, enter the Circle of Love and become like the Triune God—belong to each other, be one as our God is one, refuse to live our lives alone, and intentionally invite others into the wonder of this Circle of Love. Living in this way enables us to flourish and to reveal the goodness of the Kingdom of God to all those living on earth with us. He promises to supply all we need.

APPENDIX B
Leaders' Guide

Encourage each other in living as conquerors through this Biblical chain reaction of praise and worship, faith, prayer, overcoming evil, and reigning and ruling with Christ in His Kingdom.

The purpose of this book is to teach, encourage, and provide readers with the tools they need to be overcomers in Christ. Through story, illustration, theology, and discussion questions, readers are called to action for the purpose of integrating this chain reaction into their daily lives.

Strike the Match takes the Biblical concepts of praise and worship, faith, prayer, overcoming evil, and living in God's Kingdom, and shows how each habit ignites the next in sequence as we find ourselves in a life-transforming chain reaction.

This study is intended to promote discussion, sharing, encouragement, and learning from each other through discussing the Biblical chain reaction that is presented, digging into God's word, and finding ways that we can apply it to our lives together.

BOOK FORMAT

The five steps in the chain reaction are: Praise, Faith, Pray Powerful Prayers, Overcome Evil, and Reign and Rule with Christ. Each section (each link in the chain reaction) is presented to the reader in three chapters:

- EXAMPLES. The first chapter in each section trelates Biblical and modern-day (true) stories that illustrate this link in the chain reaction and how making it a daily habit changes lives.

- EXPLANATION. In each section, the second chapter is informational, drawing from the Bible to answer the questions: who, what, when, and where.

- APPICATION. The last chapter in each section gives Bible-based answers to the questions: why and how. It encourages and challenges participants to practice this chain reaction in their lives, to turn orthodoxy (set of beliefs) to orthopraxy (living in such a way that beliefs are evident in word and action).

- At the end of each chapter are "Explore and Exercise" pages. This study section doesn't point the reader back to the chapter for "the right answer." Instead, the questions are intended to help you:
  ◊ Think and discuss the Biblical concepts that were introduced in the chapter.
  ◊ Read about the concept through the Bible as this theme is discussed to develop greater understanding.
  ◊ Imagine how the chain reaction could work in your life and implement it today.

Some of the exercises are aimed at Biblical exploration of the theme. Some are best used for small group discussion. Often participants are asked to share things from their live, and there are always personal challenges and examples of how to incorporate the chain reaction that begins with praise into how we live our lives.

CLASS PARTICIPATION

This book is not designed to provide easy answers, but to invite people to dig in, think, and re-think. As part of the process, participants need to open our hearts to the Holy Spirit's leading so that we can find answers. While it's not a theology class, we are encouraged to explore the roots of our world and life views.

Reading the Bible isn't a once-and-done activity because it was written for the purpose of teaching (Romans 15:4). It's an ongoing conversation with God, and the Holy Spirit leads us to new insights when we engage and listen for His promptings. Because the Bible is God's word, it is referenced constantly throughout this book.

As a leader of this study, your task—should you choose to accept it—will be to serve as a discussion facilitator for the group as you explore concepts, listen to God's words, search for clear understanding, and encourage each other to take this chain reaction that God has given us and use it habitually in our lives.

> NOTE: We have found that even those who hesitate to talk in a large group will be willing to speak up in a small group of three to seven people. For this reason, we make it a practice to break into small groups (or tables) for preliminary discussions for about five to ten minutes, then have someone report from each table to the whole class.

BUILD COMMUNITY. Community is more than sitting in one room together on a Sunday morning to worship. It is relationships that develop and grow as we live our lives together—the good, the bad, and the ugly. **We all need people in our lives that we trust enough to share our lives, show our feelings, and trust each other to hold our confidences closely and with love.** This study is designed to help grow community as we celebrate others and are celebrated, as we give love and receive it, and as we serve others as they serve us.

TRUST. **What is shared in the room, stays in the room** and the hearts of those you have shared your ideas with. This is something that is worth repeating often as you meet together. We are all at different stages of spiritual maturity and circumstances, so we must respect each others' stories and testimonies and support each other. Community is built when we trust those around us.

PREPARATION. Participants are encouraged to read the material before coming to class. In addition, ask them to look through the "Explore and Exercise" section, taking time to write out answers if they so desire. However, life sometimes happens, and individuals may not have found the time to do their lesson during the week. **Encourage everyone to come whether or not they have completed the reading because discussion is an invaluable**

learning tool. No one is grading, comparing, or judging. Each person's input is vital as we grow our faith together.

SUGGESTIONS FOR LEADING A GROUP

MATERIAL. Each participant will need a copy of the book, *Strike the Match, Light the Fire*, by Kathleen Evenhouse. Bookmarks showing the chain reaction of praise (including text references) are available which can be used as a memory tool. Also available are short introductory videos for each section. Both of these items are available for purchase at www.kathleensevenhouse.com.

TIME COMMITMENT. This material fits well in a six-week class commitment. It can go longer, but adult learners often need to fit "short bursts" into their busy schedules. We chose to meet for 1½ hours.

ROOM REQUIREMENTS. Our preference has been to start with whole group introduction (or videos), discussion time in smaller groups (in same room), and return to whole group to share what we've learned. This can happen in a home setting or a classroom. Because discussion is a major learning tool in this material, we usually limit class size to 20 or less.

STRUCTURE. You know your group needs, structures, details, calendar, and facilities best, so structure the class in the way that works for you. The following are suggestions based on our experience in going through this material with a class of 15 in a six-week time period.

1. **WEEK ONE.**
   a. Pass out materials. Explain format and expectations.
   b. Have some form of group introductory mixer.
      i. We often ask people to introduce themselves and answer a few questions. For example: Do you have a come-to-Jesus story or have you had a life-long relationship with God? Why did you choose to attend this particular class?

ii. If you prefer, you can spread lengthier, more in-depth introductions over the six weeks so that everyone will get a chance. There will be a few extroverts in the first class who be willing to jump in without preparation.

c. A method that we found to be both interactive and informative is:

i. Use Teaching Video* to introduce the subject. Alternatively, on the the first week, the leader may choose to take the class through the Preface and Chapter 1 to learn the basics of the concepts.

On the following weeks, you can adapt this method to fit your class needs and schedule.

ii. Assign small groups talk through a few pages so that they can report back to whole group. Each group covers different pages of the chapter(s).

iii. Bring the whole class together to hear/discuss what each small group thought was the important learning from their assigned pages.

NOTE: We always encourage people to tell page/paragraph as they talk about what they gleaned from the material.

iv. Choose a number of discussion questions from the "Explore and Exercise" sections to discuss as a whole class.

d. If you are following a six-week class schedule, give the following assignment for the next week: Read Part 1: Praise (all three chapters) and look through the "Explore and Exercise" at the end of each chapter. (Some people will want to fill these out.)

2. **WEEK TWO.**

a. Ask for any discussion or input from last week or this week's reading.

b. Teaching Video* or read together the introduction to Praise at the beginning of the section.

c. We used a combination of large group discussion facilitated by the leader to table groups. It helps to vary the method, going back and forth between small and large groups in the way that is most effective for your class. Note: The leader can reinforce concepts by writing them down as groups report back to the entire class.

d. "Praise" and Faith are a longer sections that promote lengthy discussion. You may have carry over some discussion to the next class meeting.

e. Next week's assignment: Read Part 2: Faith (all three chapters) and look through the "Explore and Exercise" at the end of each chapter. (Some people will want to fill these out.)

The following weeks continue with a similar format.

Discussion during "Overcoming Evil" and "Reigning and Ruling" didn't seem to be as prolonged as the concepts have become familiar and understood.

Our wrap-up on Week 6 included some of "Overcoming Evil," "Reigning and Ruling," and the Overview found in Chapter 17. We also asked for any testimonies from the class in how this chain reaction had impacted their thinking, their beliefs, and their lives.

APPENDIX C
The Order of Salvation

Sanctification is an ongoing process of God and man to chop down the old nature and rebuild it with new life in Christ as we learn to imitate Him.

The life of a Christian is represented by the gray bar in the diagram. The labels are described below.

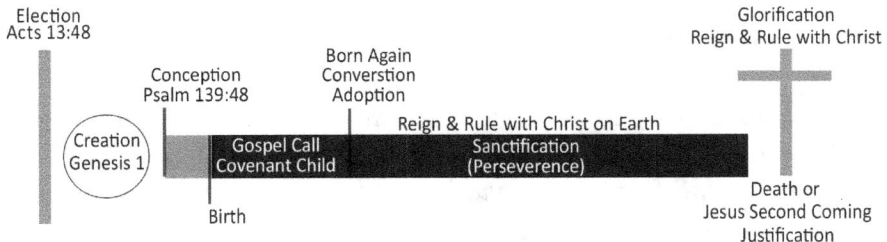

The life of a Christian is represented by the gray bar in the diagram. The labels are described below.

ELECTION, CREATION, CONCEPTION, BIRTH

Election is an act of God before creation in which he chooses some people to be saved, not on account of any foreseen merit in them, but because of his sovereign good pleasure (Genesis 1, Psalm 139:13, Acts 13:48, Romans 8:28–30, Romans 11:5–30, Ephesians 1:3–7).

> *³ All praise to God, the Father of our Lord Jesus Christ, who has blessed us with every spiritual blessing in the heavenly realms because we are united with Christ. ⁴ Even before he made the world, God loved us and chose us in Christ to be holy and without fault in his eyes. ⁵ God decided in advance to adopt us into his own family by bringing us to himself through Jesus Christ. This is what he wanted to do, and it gave him great pleasure. ⁶ So we praise God for the glorious grace he*

has poured out on us who belong to his dear Son. ⁷ He is so rich in kindness and grace that he purchased our freedom with the blood of his Son and forgave our sins. ⁸ He has showered his kindness on us, along with all wisdom and understanding (Ephesians 1:3–7, NLT).

BECOMING A CHRISTIAN

You may hear the message of the gospel **(Gospel Call)** as an ongoing call over time, as those do who are raised in a Christian home. You also may have opened your heart to God at a specific point in time **(Born Again)** in which you respond to the Holy Spirit's knock on the door of your heart and invite Him to live in you.

¹² That is why the Lord says, "Turn to me now, while there is time. Give me your hearts. Come with fasting, weeping, and mourning. ¹³ Don't tear your clothing in your grief, but tear your hearts instead." Return to the Lord your God, for he is merciful and compassionate, slow to get angry and filled with unfailing love. He is eager to relent and not punish. (Joel 2:12–13, NLT)

When you turn yourself, body and soul, over to God **(Conversion)**, you repent and go forward in faith (See also: Psalm 51:3-4, Ephesians 1:13-14).

¹⁷ This means that anyone who belongs to Christ has become a new person. The old life is gone; a new life has begun! (2 Corinthians 5:17, NLT)

NOW AND NOT YET

God's Kingdom on earth **(now)** as it will be in heaven for eternity **(not yet)**.

(NOW) JUSTIFICATION.

You are brought to a right legal standing in God's judgment because Christ paid the penalty for our sins. This is how God views you (NOW) as you live in God's Kingdom here on earth. It is also a specific point in time (NOT YET)—when you stand before his throne at your death or His second coming (John 3:16-21).

(NOW) ADOPTION

You have been adopted as a member of God's family (John 1:12-13.)

(NOW) SANCTIFICATION

Sanctification is an ongoing process of God and man to chop down the old nature and rebuild it with new life in Christ as we learn to imitate him. This process takes place throughout our entire lifetime (Ephesians 4:21-24, 1 Corinthians 1:18, Philippians 1:6).

> *Since you have heard about Jesus and have learned the truth that comes from him,* ^{22} *throw off your old sinful nature and your former way of life, which is corrupted by lust and deception.* ^{23} *Instead, let the Spirit renew your thoughts and attitudes.* ^{24} **Put on your new nature, created** *to be like God—truly righteous and holy.* (Ephesians 4:21–24, NLT)

(NOW) PERSEVERANCE AS WE REIGN AND RULE IN GOD'S KINGDOM ON EARTH

Perseverance is your part in the sanctification process in which you daily give up your soulish nature and give the Holy Spirit control of your soul, body, and actions (Philippians 2:13-14, John 15:55, Colossians 3:1-10).

> ^{5} *"Yes, I am the vine; you are the branches. Those who remain in me, and I in them, will produce much fruit. For apart from me you can do nothing.* (John 15:5, NLT)

(NOT YET) DEATH OR CHRIST'S SECOND COMING

When we die or Christ returns, we will face judgment.

> ^{26} *Then everyone will see the Son of Man coming on the clouds with great power and glory.* ^{27} *And he will send out his angels to gather his chosen ones from all over the world—from the farthest ends of the earth and heaven.* ^{28} *"Now learn a lesson from the fig tree. When its branches bud and its leaves begin to sprout, you know that summer is near.* ^{29} *In the same way, when you see all these things taking place, you can know that his return is very near, right at the*

door. ³¹ Heaven and earth will disappear, but my words will never disappear. ³² "However, no one knows the day or hour when these things will happen, not even the angels in heaven or the Son himself. Only the Father knows. ³³ And since you don't know when that time will come, be on guard! Stay alert!" (Mark 13:31–33, NLT)

(NOT YET) GLORIFICATION

We will receive a resurrection body and reign and rule with Jesus in heaven (1 Corinthians 15:53, Romans 8:10-11, 1 Corinthians 15:44, 1 Corinthians 15:50–57).

⁵⁰ What I am saying, dear brothers and sisters, is that our physical bodies cannot inherit the Kingdom of God. These dying bodies cannot inherit what will last forever. ⁵¹ But let me reveal to you a wonderful secret. We will not all die, but we will all be transformed! ⁵² It will happen in a moment, in the blink of an eye, when the last trumpet is blown. For when the trumpet sounds, those who have died will be raised to live forever. And we who are living will also be transformed. ⁵³ For our dying bodies must be transformed into bodies that will never die; our mortal bodies must be transformed into immortal bodies. ⁵⁴ Then, when our dying bodies have been transformed into bodies that will never die, this Scripture will be fulfilled: "Death is swallowed up in victory. ⁵⁵ O death, where is your victory? O death, where is your sting?" ⁵⁶ For sin is the sting that results in death, and the law gives sin its power. ⁵⁷ But thank God! He gives us victory over sin and death through our Lord Jesus Christ. (1 Corinthians 15:50–57, NLT)

You are brought to a right legal standing in God's judgment because Christ paid the penalty for our sins. This is how God views you (NOW) as you live in God's Kingdom here on earth. It is also a specific point in time (NOT YET)—when you stand before his throne at your death or His second coming (John 3:16-21).

APPENDIX D

The Will of God

God's will encompasses our entire being and life—not just our death—and extends to eternity.

In a small, easy-to-read book of five sermons entitled *The Will of God*, London pastor, Leslie Weatherhead, suggests that the phrase "the will of God" is used so loosely that we can be confused about what this term means. Weatherhead describes "God's will" with three distinctions:

INTENTIONAL WILL

God's ideal plan for man—his original creation

Long before he laid down earth's foundations, he had us in mind, had settled on us as the focus of his love, to be made whole and holy by his love. (Ephesians 1:4, MSG)

God created a perfect world with God and man interacting in harmony. God gave humankind the freedom to choose beliefs, thoughts, words, and actions, even though He knew that eventually someone would make a bad choice, and evil would enter the world.

CIRCUMSTANTIAL WILL

God's plan within the circumstances in which we experience life in this sinful world

He is so rich in kindness and grace that he purchased our freedom with the blood of his Son and forgave our sins. (Ephesians 1:7, NLT)

No, the wisdom we speak of is the mystery of God—his plan that was previously hidden, even though he made it for our ultimate glory before the world began. (1 Corinthians 2:7, NLT)

God had Jesus in mind to handle the evil circumstances that would result from our sinful choices. Jesus' painful death and resurrection, which paid for our sins and guaranteed our redemption, wasn't God's intentional will, but his circumstantial will. God didn't plan evil or intend evil for the world; that burden lies at the feet of humanity.

When circumstances eat away at our lives, it can appear to us that evil is winning. Pastor Weatherhead describes the reaction of Jesus' disciples after his death: "On Good Friday night eleven men, in the deepest gloom, felt like you. They said in their hearts: 'We trusted Him; we followed Him; it was His will to establish His kingdom. He told us so. And evil has been allowed to take Him from us. It's the end of everything.' But they were wrong, weren't they? It was only the end of their mistake and the beginning of the most wonderful use of evil which God has ever effected."

ULTIMATE WILL

God's final realization of His purposes to bring man back into harmony with him in eternity.

No one's ever seen or heard anything like this, never so much as imagined anything quite like it—what God has arranged for those who love him. (1 Corinthians 2:9, MSG)

God's intentional plan was obstructed by sinful choices, but through His circumstantial will, Jesus died to pay for the sins of each and every one of us, and God's ultimate will is realized—the victory is already won. We are brought back to unity with Him.

God's will encompasses our entire being and life—not just our death—and extends to eternity. Trust God. God is love. Rest in His nature and His will for you.

Scripture Index

OLD TESTAMENT

• Genesis •
Genesis 1 .... 108, 183, 247
Genesis 3 .... 36, 79, 157
Genesis 9 211
Genesis 18 136

• Exodus •
Exodus 14 83

• Deuteronomy •
Deuteronomy 6 165
Deuteronomy 7 193
Deuteronomy 11 .... 79, 80, 81
Deuteronomy 31 90

• Judges •
Judges 6-7 .... 61, 62, 67

• Ruth •
Ruth 1-4 14
Ruth 1 .... 18, 185

• 1 & 2 Samuel •
1 Samuel 1 136
2 Samuel 6 38
2 Samuel 7 110
1 Samuel 10 39
2 Samuel 11 32
1 Samuel 13-14 .... 145, 152
1 Samuel 16 .... 33, 196
1 Samuel 18 145
2 Samuel 22 196

• 1 & 2 Kings •
1 Kings 1 21
1 Kings 15-16 24
1 Kings 18 126
2 Kings 3 38
2 Kings 5 832
2 Kings 6 166

• 1 & 2 Chronicles •
1 Chronicles 23 72
1 Chronicles 25 39
2 Chronicles 7 180
2 Chronicles 10-12 23
2 Chronicles 14 24
2 Chronicles 20 .... 21, 24, 49
.... 91, 113, 209

• Job •

Job 13
Job 2 159
Job 38 108

• Psalms •

Psalm 8: 19, 48, 55, 70, 183
Psalm 10 117
Psalm 18 74
Psalm 22 .... 19, 56
Psalm 16 177
Psalm 23 .... 47, 48, 54
Psalm 27 193
Psalm 28 38
Psalm 31 32
Psalm 32 14
Psalm 34 211
Psalm 37 19
Psalm 40 39
Psalm 42 .... 21, 40
Psalm 46 .... 3, 50
Psalm 47 492
Psalm 50 40
Psalm 51 .... 33, 36, 248
Psalm 57 38
Psalm 62 93
Psalm 72 40
Psalm 73 42
Psalm 91 30
Psalm 103 193
Psalm 104 129
Psalms 113-118 43
Psalm 117 40
Psalm 119 .... 111, 196
Psalm 149 38
Psalm 138 37
Psalm 139 247

• Proverbs •

Proverbs 3 116
Proverbs 6 0196

• Ecclesiastes •

Ecclesiastes 1 IX

• Isaiah •

Isaiah 3 121
Isaiah 26 212
Isaiah 40 193
Isaiah 43 91
Isaiah 52 173
Isaiah 61 135

• Jeremiah •

Jeremiah 29 239

• Lamentations •

Lamentations 3 193

• Ezekiel •

Ezekiel 22 .... 124, 180

• Daniel •

Daniel 6 110

Daniel 10 .... 161, 166

• **Joel** •

Joel 2 .... 105, 134, 248

• **Habbakuk** •

Habbakuk 2 133

NEW TESTAMENT

• **Matthew** •

Matthew 3 127
Matthew 5 ...... 202, 213, 214, 221
Matthew 6 104
Matthew 7 .... 135, 228
Matthew 8 49
Matthew 10 76
Matthew 11 .... 127, 193, 213
Matthew 14 .... 70, 82
Matthew 18 .... 135, 214
Matthew 19 115
Matthew 21 82
Matthew 22 112
Matthew 25 .... 195, 202, 206
Matthew 26-27 .... 14, 103, 110
Matthew 28 .... 156, 200

• **Mark** •

Mark 1 115
Mark 9 .... 71, 113, 162, 212
Mark 10 202
Mark 11 .... 110, 212
Mark 12 204

Mark 13 249
Mark 14 .... 116, 229
Mark 16 14

• **Luke** •

Luke 1 76
Luke 2 187
Luke 8 .... 14, 195
Luke 9 135
Luke 10 .... 19, 156, 188
Luke 11 156
Luke 12 195
Luke 18 101
Luke 19 73
Luke 22 .... 126, 158
Luke 24 .... 52, 70, 199

• **John** •

John 1 .... 117, 211, 219, 249
John 2 212
John 3 .... 14, 108, 125, 193, 211
.... 238, 248
John 4 180
John 6 76
John 8 .... 76, 157
John 10 .... 76, 126, 211
John 11 14
John 12 .... 158, 159
John 14 ...... IV, 117, 162, 196, 212
John 15 .... 16, 214, 238, 249

John 16............ 143, 158, 211, 250
John 17.................... 126, 204, 229
John 18....................................202
John 20....................................156
John 21....................................103

• **Acts** •

Acts 1 103, 174, 199, 200, 207, 211
Acts 2..................... 126, 133, 188
Acts 3.....................................112
Acts 4.....................................129
Acts 6.....................................103
Acts 9............................. 124, 189
Acts 10................ 95, 97, 103, 196
Acts 11....................................175
Acts 12............... 83, 98, 104. 129
Acts 13............................ 113, 247
Acts 16....................... 54, 83, 175
Acts 27......................................89
Acts 28.............................90, 200

• **Romans** •

Romans 1 .... 14. 48, 56, 129
Romans 4 213
Romans 5 48
Romans 6 193
Romans 7 .... 159, 165
Romans 8 ..... 76, 91, 93, 116. 126
.... 212, 222, 230, 238, 247, 250
Romans 9 196
Romans 11 .... 35, 247
Romans 12 .... X, 19, 71, 156
.... 167, 170, 174, 215, 229
Romans 13 167
Romans 14........................ 15, 76
Romans 15 .... 128, 242
Romans 16 175

• **1 & 2 Corinthians** •

1 Corinthians 1.............. 109, 249
1 Corinthians 2..... 202, 251, 252
I Corinthians 3 76
1 Corinthians 4.....................211
1 Corinthians 6..50, 76, 115, 205
1 Corinthians 10..... 35, 172, 173
1 Corinthians 12........... 112, 133
....202, 206
1 Corinthians 13............. 41, 202
1 Corinthians 14....110, 112, 133
1 Corinthians 15...................250
2 Corinthians 1....... 76, 120, 212
2 Corinthians 2............. 158, 194
2 Corinthians 4............ 155, 157
.... 158. 159
2 Corinthians 5............. 209, 248
2 Corinthians 10....................172
2 Corinthians 11....................157
2 Corinthians 12....................212